GH00992039

Assemblies for Primary Schools

Autumn Term

Margaret Cooling

ASSOCIATION OF CHRISTIAN TEACHERS

RELIGIOUS AND MORAL EDUCATION PRESS

ASSEMBLIES FOR PRIMARY SCHOOLS: AUTUMN TERM

Religious and Moral Education Press
An imprint of Chansitor Publications Ltd,
a wholly owned subsidiary of Hymns Ancient & Modern Ltd of
St Mary's Works, St Mary's Plain
Norwich, Norfolk NR3 3BH

First published 1990
Reprinted 1991, 1994

ISBN 0 900274 58 1 spiral
0 900274 59 X paperback

Printed in Great Britain by
BPC Wheatons Ltd, Exeter

CONTENTS

Group D: Autumn festivals

Group E: The Disciples

Group F: Prayer

Group G: Forgiveness

Group H: Christmas

ACKNOWLEDGEMENTS

I would like to thank my husband Trevor for writing a substantial portion of the Introduction and for his help, support and advice in the writing of this book.

I would also like to thank Margaret Woodhall for her research work and Patricia Dorbin for her helpful comments on these assemblies.

I am indebted to the primary schools of Stapleford who have experienced many of these assemblies, and our sons Robert and Terence on whom many of the ideas were tried out. I am also indebted to Arthur Rowe whose thinking was a source of inspiration.

My thanks also to my mother who not only contributed ideas but supported the whole family during the writing process.

Many of the ideas in this book were developed at Stapleford House, the Training Centre of the Association of Christian Teachers. Stapleford House regularly runs courses on assemblies and R.E. Further details can be obtained from: Stapleford House, Wesley Place, Stapleford, Nottingham NG9 8DP.

The extract on p.63 from 'King John's Christmas' by A.A. Milne is reproduced by permission of Methuen Ltd.

The musical notation for 'Amazing Grace' on p.79 is reproduced from *Sing, Clap and Play* by H. Cox and G. Rickard, published by Macmillan.

The story on p.81 is based on 'The Legend of the Spider's Web' by William Barclay.

INTRODUCTION

The place of collective worship in the primary school has been firmly established by the 1988 Education Act. Each school has to provide a minimum of 190 assemblies a year; a few schools may well have to organize over a thousand a year – no mean feat when it is considered that a good assembly can take over an hour to plan. This book is designed to help already overstretched primary teachers understand and fulfil their responsibilities in this area.

The Requirements of the 1988 Act

The Act lays down a number of requirements on school worship. These include:

1. There must be a *daily* act of worship for *all* pupils at the school and this should take place on the school's premises. This can be at any time of the day, but does not have to be a gathering of the *whole* school together. A number of acts of worship can take place in any one school on any one day, as long as the pupils are in a normal teaching group or a group which exists for other school activities. A group cannot reflect the beliefs of a particular religious tradition. [However, see point 5 following]

2. Parents may withdraw their children from acts of worship and teachers may also opt out of participating in them.

3. Most acts of worship in a term are to be 'wholly or mainly of a broadly Christian character'. An act of worship is considered to be of a broadly Christian character if it 'reflects the broad traditions of Christian belief without being distinctive of any particular Christian denomination'.

4. In planning broadly Christian worship, schools are required to ensure that such acts are appropriate for their pupils, taking into account considerations of:
   • circumstances relating to the family background of the pupils concerned;
   • the ages and aptitudes of the pupils.

5. If headteachers feel that such broadly Christian worship is not appropriate for some or all of their pupils they can, after consulting with their governing body, apply to their local Standing Advisory Council on Religious Education for what is called a determination. This means that they can arrange other acts of worship, which are not of a broadly Christian character for some or all of their pupils. These acts may be distinctive of a particular religious *faith* but they cannot be distinctive of a particular religious *denomination*.

1

6. The responsibility for worship arrangements lies with the headteacher after consultation with the governing body.

The arrangements for Church and other voluntary schools are slightly different. In these cases the character of the worship should be in accordance with the school's trust deed and the final responsibility for the arrangements rests with the governing body, after consultation with the headteacher.

Government Circulations

In 1994, the Government issued two circulars (number 1/94 in England and 10/94 in Wales) offering schools an interpretation of the legal requirements contained in the 1988 Education Act. The following points were particularly important:

(a) Worship was given a more precise definition. Summed up, the circulars said that this must involve veneration or reverence paid to a divine being or power and that it should be something special or separate from ordinary school activities.

(b) The circulars said that pupils should be given the opportunity to worship God. The emphasis was on pupil participation.

(c) It was stated that broadly Christian worship must contain elements which reflect the special status Jesus Christ has in Christian belief.

These requirements generated an angry reaction from many people who felt they were inappropriate in modern schools. However there were other elements in the circulars which suggested that this concern for appropriateness had not been ignored. In particular:

(a) There was a considerable emphasis given to the requirement that school worship should be appropriate for all children irrespective of their family background. School worship was not to be the same as that which happens in a group with beliefs in common.

(b) A distinction was introduced between taking part, which all pupils should be able to do, and actively identifying with the act of worship, which not all pupils may be able to do.

(c) The importance of a number of features that are traditionally part of primary school assemblies was re-affirmed. These included consideration of spiritual and moral issues, developing community spirit and promoting a common ethos and shared values.

The difficulty for schools lies in combining the more explicitly religious and Christian features in my first list with the broader requirements in the second list.

Added to the difficulties of implementing the requirements of the law, is the concern generated by the fact that worship is part of the inspection process. It is important to realize that inspectors are sympathetic to the challenges schools face in this area. Of course they have to report if a school is failing to fulfil the law, for example by not providing daily worship for every child. They will however also report positively if schools are promoting the spiritual, moral, cultural and social development of pupils even if all the legal requirements are not being met.

The suggestions that follow are an attempt to plot one course through the maze of legal requirement and educational aspiration.

The Problems

The requirements for Christian worship have been criticized in some quarters as Christian imperialism. For example, early in 1989 the Muslim Educational Trust issued a pamphlet saying Muslim children will be required 'to pray to Jesus as the Son of God, learn about the Trinity and thus commit the awesome sin of Shirk, associating others with Allah. This is the worst thing a Muslim can do.' They therefore advised Muslim parents to withdraw their children from school worship. Teachers will need to be aware of the difficulties that can be caused for some parents by the requirement that worship be broadly Christian.

The second problem is both practical and ethical. Clearly children cannot be compelled to worship. Bitter experience of 600 children refusing to sing a hymn in an Easter service convinced me of that very early in my teaching career. Even if worship could be compelled it certainly should *not* be. Just because infants can be made unquestioningly to pray to Jesus does not mean that such activity is legitimate.

However, despite the problems associated with worship, educationally we cannot do without it. There are two reasons why this is the case.

Firstly, experience of stillness, peace, awe, wonder, mystery, celebration, reverence and belonging are of central importance in promoting spiritual development. In a school day, and indeed in most children's lives, school worship will be one of the few contexts where such experiences can be explored and reflected upon.

Secondly, religious beliefs and practices may appear simply as odd people doing and believing odd things unless there is some experiential under-standing of what belief means to the believer. Without school worship there will be little opportunity to give children the 'feels that make the tolds fall into place' in the religious realm. It provides a unique opportunity to help children become more aware of the importance of the human search for meaning in the face of life's mysteries.

Planning worship is rather like being asked to plot a course through a minefield. There will be mishaps on the way and it will no doubt be a hair-raising experience, but the satisfaction and rewards of reaching the other side are enormous. Successful school worship can provide some of those special moments for both teachers and pupils.

Some Ways through the Minefield

In order to make a success of school worship I would suggest that the following principles are adopted.

(a) *Distinguish between assembly and worship*

For years we have been used to conflating these two activities and school worship has been equated with any act of gathering together of the school.

Circulars 1/94 and 10/94 make it quite plain that these two activities are distinct. Teachers are bound by contract to attend assembly; however, they have the right to opt out of worship.

The gathering of the school community in an assembly for administration and other purposes is an important activity, but it does not have to take place every day. Religious worship does, however, have to be a daily act. In these notes I shall ignore the question of the secular assembly, understood as a purely administrational or community building event, my comments are addressed solely to the activity of *worship*. Even so, I shall still use the word *assembly* to describe the act of religious worship, since this is the word most commonly used by teachers. Its specific and particular use in this book should always be remembered.

(b) *Be aware of the dangers*

One important way of avoiding mines is to be aware of their presence in advance. There are five that are the most frequent causes of explosion in school worship.

(i) *Compromising pupil integrity*

This is what Muslim parents quite rightly object to. Christian parents are equally incensed when their children are invited to make offerings to a Hindu goddess in the name of multiculturalism. Many parents who are not religious themselves are deeply offended when schools assume that their children will, for example, pray to Jesus. The sensitivities of parents vary enormously in this respect, but it is quite wrong for schools to expect them to bury their deepest convictions for the sake of some educational ideal. Children should not be required to compromise their integrity through involvement in acts of school worship.

(ii) *Misrepresenting religious faith*

This is another cause of offence to religious communities. The two most common manifestations in school are syncretism and relativism. Syncretism is when an attempt is made to unify different religions. Relativism is when religions are treated as culturally specific – for example, when it is implied that Islam is true for Arabs whereas Christianity is true for Westerners. Schools have fallen into both of these traps in their attempts to produce non-divisive, multicultural acts of worship. It is a mistake, however, to think that a sense of community can be fostered by arranging acts of worship that may turn out to be offensive to particular religious minorities.

This is not to say that syncretism or relativism are wrong, indeed they are positions taken by some religions. What is wrong is for schools to assume them as given. It is equally a mistake, although a less common practice, for schools to imply that all genuine religions are exclusive, claiming to be the only way to God.

(iii) *Messages from reluctant staff*

Most teachers can remember assemblies from their own school days which were led by teachers who clearly didn't believe in what they were doing. These memories should be enough to ensure that we never put fellow teachers in the position of leading worship when they feel compromised by such an act. Particular care over this will need to be exercised by schools which arrange for worship to take place in class or form groups.

(iv) *Trivializing the spiritual*

Many adults will also have memories of being harangued by the headteacher about graffiti in the toilets or litter on the field, just after having sung a hymn about the love of God. To imply, by association, that God is on the side of school rules or that He cares ultimately about the success of the football or netball team is to trivialize the spiritual realm. This is one very good reason for having a clear separation in teachers' minds between secular assemblies and religious worship. It may be a very good reason for physically separating the two events.

(v) *Organizing inappropriate worship*

The law is quite clear that worship must be appropriate for the very mixed population of children present in most schools in Britain. All schools will have minorities of pupils belonging to families who are active members of faith communities. The vast majority of pupils will come from homes which are largely secularized. This makes the 'congregation' very different from that in church. The challenge of providing appropriate worship for children from secularized backgrounds is very different from that facing any Christian minister or Sunday School leader. If failure or large numbers of withdrawals are to be avoided, schools will have to think in very different terms from those employed by people organizing worship in the Christian community. School and church are not the same. This is why the Act refers to collective worship as opposed to corporate worship. The latter is an activity that can take place only amongst people who have shared religious beliefs.

(c) *Think carefully abut the meaning of worship*

Worship is usually seen as adoration of God by a group of believers who are in voluntary association. Such a view makes it a totally inappropriate activity for a school whose members are compelled to be there and who represent a variety of different faith positions. Unless we can develop a broader understanding of worship it has little future as a school-based activity. No amount of legal compulsion will overcome the ethical and religious objections.

In fact, even amongst a group of committed believers, a wide variety of *responses* will be in evidence during any one act of worship. The range of these is illustrated in the list below, which is by no means exhaustive:

- awareness of
- appreciation of
- respect for
- preference for
- commitment to
- devotion to
- adoration of.

This diversity of response indicates a way forward for worship in schools. Worship is offensive only if pupils are compelled to respond in a particular way. If acts of worship can be designed which leave pupils free to respond in any of the seven ways listed above, then the main problem of compulsory worship is overcome. One of the chief questions in the minds of those planning acts of worship should therefore be whether this activity leaves pupils free to respond in a way that is appropriate for them given their family background or whether it compels and expects one type of response only. The former should always be the case. No presumptions should be made on behalf of pupils.

Another way forward is to consider exactly what *activities* are associated with worship. Traditionally prayer, hymn singing and readings from sacred texts have been seen to characterize worship. Again I would argue that this is an unnecessarily narrow conception. A number of other activities can legitimately be called worship. Amongst these are:

- reflection on the meaning and purpose of life
- pondering ultimate questions
- developing a sense of transcendence
- responding to challenge
- experiential exploration of a religious idea
- celebration of learning about religion
- learning from the experience of others.

All these are legitimate educational activities, and when combined with an approach which gives freedom of pupil response, they present a very positive formula for thinking about school worship.

Practically, what has been said in this section amounts to two priorities for the teacher.

(i) Consideration should be given to the language that is used when conducting worship. Inclusive language such as 'we believe that' or 'we will all pray' should be avoided in favour of language that grounds beliefs in a particular faith tradition. To return to the Muslim concern mentioned earlier, it is quite wrong to say that Jesus is the Son of God, but legitimate to ask children to reflect on *the Christian belief* that Jesus is the Son of God. The former insists on assent, the latter presents a belief which the children are free to respond to in their own way, even if that response only amounts to an awareness that this belief is important to Christians.

(ii) Consideration should also be given to allowing pupils to function comfortably in worship secure in a sense of their own religious identity. For younger pupils this will be derived from their family, for older ones it may be much more a matter of their own personal conviction. Worship should be so structured that each pupil can be comfortable either with the notion that this activity is an adventure into something that he or she identifies with or alternatively that it is an exploration into something that is 'not me'. Here exploration does not imply assent. Respecting pupil identity should be of paramount importance in preparing worship and the demands will be different depending on the type of school and the nature of the community it serves.

(d) *Making worship 'broadly Christian'*

This particular phraseology has been hedged about with several qualifiers. What exactly is meant by this is as yet unclear. Even 'experts' in R.E. cannot decide what is meant. There are, however, three things that are very clear from the Act.

First, broadly Christian worship in schools is not the same as distinctively or uniquely Christian worship. So, such acts of worship can include material drawn from non-Christian, and even non-religious, traditions provided that, taken as a whole, they reflect the traditions of Christian belief.

Secondly, broadly Christian worship has to reflect the broad traditions of Christian *belief*, not the broad traditions of Christian *worship*. This is a significant statement because the word 'belief' is not the one that would most readily spring to mind when framing such a clause. School worship is to be a communal exploration of beliefs in a manner appropriate for schoolchildren and not a kaleidoscope of the practices of Christian adults from a variety of church backgrounds. However, this is not to imply that school worship should consist of monologues on particular doctrines! Experiential approaches are essential and it is most important to stimulate the affective as well as the cognitive. So, for example, in an assembly on creation, children should come to feel awe and wonder and not just be told about it.

Thirdly, worship will *reflect* the broad traditions of Christian belief. It is not required that these beliefs by systematically expounded or affirmed or even that they form the central focus of the act of worship. It is only necessary that they be reflected in what happens.

I would suggest that there are two understandings of the phrase 'broadly Christian' which can be profitably developed:

(i) There are many values and beliefs which are part of the broad traditions of Christian belief but which are also widely held in society at large. Examples include a sense of awe at the natural world and the merits of sacrificial love. Such values can be explored and celebrated in school worship in a manner that complements the way they are taught in the classroom and communicated through the ethos of the school.

(ii) There are various concepts which are central to traditional Christian belief. Examples include reconciliation, incarnation and creation. Such beliefs are shared across Christian denominations and can therefore legitimately form a focus for school worship, as long as what we have already said about freedom of pupil response is kept clearly in mind.

Conclusion

The function of this book is to help the busy primary school teacher fulfil the major requirements of the 1988 Education Act in relation to school worship. The acts of worship in the book are designed to be appropriate to primary age children, using the children's experience to explore Christian belief. They are either of a *wholly* or of a *mainly* broadly Christian character and the teacher will have to decide which can be used in the particular context of his or her school. Some of the material may be felt to be appropriate only in church schools, but the vast majority of it can be used in most schools as long as the teachers are sensitive to the needs and background of their children. Follow-up work is suggested so that worship and classroom work can be integrated.

Our hope is that teachers will be able to use these ideas to organize acts of worship which enable children to learn from Christian belief in a way that promotes their spiritual, moral, cultural and social development.

PRACTICAL GUIDANCE

In the Introduction to this book I have examined the legal and educational context in which school worship takes place. In this section I shall suggest a series of 'dos and don'ts' to which teachers and others can refer in the planning of school worship. Individual teachers may wish to add guidelines of their own. This is followed by some practical guidance on the use of this book.

Dos and Don'ts

There are various pitfalls to be avoided when taking assemblies. Below are a few suggestions of things to beware of.

Dos and don'ts for teachers taking Christian assemblies

1. Avoid tying religious faith with the children's behaviour too tightly. Of course there is a close connection between faith and action but faith should never be used to manipulate. Children rightly resent such attempts. Religious faith should be seen as something that changes both the child's and the adult's behaviour. Religious faith should not be used to bolster school rules.

Example: Good Christians do not run in the corridor or drop litter.

2. Do not put people in a corner. Both adults and children need to feel that their identity is protected. Use a non-offensive phrase such as 'Christians believe' or 'Jesus said'. Do not say 'You should…' or 'We all…'. The use of non-offensive phrases allows people emotionally to opt in or to opt out of an assembly. It allows people to decide their attitude to an assembly and either identify with the faith being explored or explore that faith from a greater distance. With very young children there is obviously a difficulty of understanding such phrases, but even so safeguards need building in.

3. Do speak to their world. Even in the short space of an assembly the rule of starting where the children are and finishing where they are not still applies. Start from the known to lead children to the unknown. Move from the familiar to the unfamiliar.

Example: A simple transformer or the use of the dressing-up box can start a child thinking about changes. You can then lead them on to thinking about changing on the inside.

4. Don't make comments about other faiths, agnostics or atheists.

5. Don't go into highly controversial areas. Assembly is not the place for controversy. No one can disagree with you if you are taking the assembly and the rest of the staff might feel you are abusing your platform.

6. Don't be denominational. The law allows you to be Christian but not denominational in an act of worship. It is better for the children if Christians share their agreements rather than dwell on their differences.

7. Be aware of the dangers of raising areas of pastoral concern unless you have been specifically asked to do so. Such areas need careful preparation and follow-up by all the staff. Subjects such as war, death, divorce and similar matters are generally better dealt with in a pastoral situation.

8. Don't make casual allusions that are not followed up. Asides confuse children. Stick very strictly to the subject and do not deviate from it.

9. Assemblies are very short and children understand things better if they come in small parcels. Choose one small area and deal with it well rather than ranging over a large subject.

10. Do not make children pray, instead ask them to listen while you pray or read a prayer. An acceptable formula might be something like this:
   'I am going to pray (or read a Christian prayer). I would like you to keep very still, close your eyes and listen carefully to the words. Those of you who wish to can join in with the Amen (I agree) at the end.'
In this way children are not joining in Christian prayers against their will, but they are listening respectfully and possibly thinking about the prayer.

11. If you use hymns and songs remember to think carefully about the words, in the light of some of the dangers of worship already described. For example, singing the song 'Jesus is Lord' would be inappropriate in many situations.

Dos and don'ts for visitors taking Christian assemblies

All the dos and don'ts for teachers apply to visitors but there are some extra ones which are also relevant.

1. Do be friendly and polite. This should go without saying. Thank the school for inviting you and treat both the staff and pupils with respect.

2. Do realize you are a guest and probably not there by right. There should be no attitude of infiltrating enemy territory! Visitors serve the school as part of the community and *vice versa*. Visitor participation in assemblies should be seen as a learning partnership on both sides. Both should be open to criticism and praise. The school should be able to cope with the occasional disaster and help the visitor to learn from their mistakes. The visitor must be open to such positive criticism.

3. Accept a healthy suspicion on the part of the school. This is part of their pastoral role, appreciate the fact that they do not let just anybody in to take assemblies. Offer references if necessary, someone who knows how you

relate to children. Offer to let the headteacher see what you are going to say beforehand if he or she wishes to.

4. Do remember that the children do not volunteer for assembly. You can help them explore Christianity but do not 'push' faith in an inappropriate way.

5. Remember it is a school not a church; do not assume belief or familiarity with Christianity or biblical stories.

6. Do bear in mind the Christian members of staff. You can either be a great encouragement to them or make life difficult. Remember it is they who will hear the comments in the staffroom.

7. Make sure you manage the practical details well. Organize the time, date, venue and duration of the assembly. Make sure you know the age group of the children you are talking to. Telephone the school a day or so beforehand to reassure them that you are coming and to make any necessary arrangements.

8. Do make visual aids and writing large enough to be seen from the back. Small pictures, tiny writing and small objects will cause the children to start kneeling up to see and they will soon lose interest in what they cannot see.

9. Do not undermine the school in the remarks that you make.

Example: We all know how horrible school dinners are.

10. Don't make sexist or racist comments. Take the same care over your language as teachers do. Ask girls to help as well as boys. Encourage girls as well as boys to answer questions. Are all your main characters white and male or are some of them girls or black or handicapped?

11. Remember that sight reading is an adult skill. If you are going to teach the children a song or have something for them to read, do help them. Fluency in reading does not come until the middle junior years and for some it comes much later. Read things with children. Always print in lower case letters, never capitals.

NOTE: Detailed guidance on visitors taking Christian assemblies can be found in the books *Your Turn to Take Assembly* by Howard Cunnington, published by ACT (available from ACT, 2 Romeland Hill, St Albans, Herts. AL3 4ET) and *Leading School Worship* by Janet King, published by Monarch.

Dos and don'ts for the school that invites visitors in to take assembly

1. Do be polite and helpful. Many teachers are so busy that visitors are sometimes left feeling abandoned. Make sure they have the equipment and information they need.

2. Do arrange for someone to meet a visitor. It is very unnerving to walk into a school and not be able to find the head or secretary.

3. Do introduce and thank a visitor.

4. Do brief a visitor well. They need to know the situation they are coming into and what you are happy for them to do.

5. Do check visitors. Not all visitors are suitable for taking assemblies.

6. Do phone the visitor beforehand to confirm that they are coming.

7. If your school sings hymns do give the visitor a hymn book. They can feel very silly standing silently in front of three hundred singing children.

8. Be positive in your criticism, but be honest. Be prepared for the occasional disaster, but treat it as a joint learning experience.

Using the Material

This book is concerned with leading Christian assemblies, but tries to recognize the stress that such assemblies can put on staff. The following features have therefore been included:

Seventy assemblies

There are seventy assemblies in this book, which approximately reflects the length of the autumn term. A school can choose what percentage of Christian assemblies they wish to use from this collection to contribute towards the Christian input into their assembly programme.

School weeks

The assemblies are blocked in groups of five, ten and fifteen so that they fit in with a five-day school week pattern.

Longer themes

The assemblies are blocked in themes so that one theme covers a whole week, fortnight or month. This allows teachers to explore an idea in depth rather than doing a variety of 'one offs'. If any theme is too long for your school it can be split into smaller groups or individual assemblies.

Active assemblies

As far as possible the assemblies involve the children in active exploration of their own experience. Normal classroom practice is carried over into assemblies so that teachers can use familiar techniques with the children who are encouraged to join in. Because the assemblies involve interaction with the children every word of an assembly cannot be written out. Suitable questions are indicated, but obviously the way the conversation develops depends on the pupils' contribution.

A variety of material

All the assemblies are broadly Christian but some deal with issues that are more centrally Christian than others. This variety is provided to allow as many teachers as possible to take part without feeling that their own position is compromised. Some teachers, for example, might be happy taking an assembly on the Good Samaritan but would be uncomfortable taking an assembly on Easter.

A variety of methods

These assemblies use a variety of methods: drama, storytelling, games and art. Teachers can select from the assemblies the type of material they feel confident in handling.

Preparation

We recognize the pressures on teachers and have tried to keep preparation down to the minimum. Most of what would be called preparation is actually done in the assembly 'Blue Peter' style so that you do not have to have things ready prepared. To save further time we recommend that an 'Assembly Box' be kept in the staff room with most of the basic materials you will need to execute these assemblies.

The Assembly Box

This is a storage box (a cardboard box will do) that contains basic materials such as card, paper and pens. The contents should be checked regularly against a list stuck to the outside. If possible appoint an older child to check the box once a week.

Other items which are needed for a particular assembly can be brought in by the teacher or the pupils. Wherever possible delegate what preparation there is by asking a child or an adult helper to make sure that you have in the box what you need for your specific assembly by checking the 'You will need' section of the assembly against the contents of the assembly box.

Contents of the assembly box:

1. Pritt stick
2. Sugar paper
3. A4 paper
4. Large sheets of paper (lining paper or the back of wallpaper will do)
5. Scissors
6. Card (offcuts left over from art classes and some A4)
7. Blu-Tak
8. Several balls of coloured wool
9. Felt pens, large and small
10. If you use an overhead projector (OHP), acetates and pens will be needed.

Health and safety

All paints and glues used should be non-toxic. Any scissors used should be the safe variety normally used in primary schools. If you decide to light any candles this should be done only by an adult with due regard to safety and they should be blown out so that any decorations or greenery are not ignited. All activities should be carried out with a normal regard for safety.

Language

The language of the assemblies has been kept as simple as possible, but infant/nursery teachers might feel they need to adapt the language further.

Passages from the Bible have been paraphrased or adapted. Although they are true to the message or meaning of a passage, they are not a direct or literal translation.

'Think about it' sections

These sections have been included to allow children a time of reflection and quietness. Teachers can decide whether or not they are suitable for their school. The time of reflection can be ended with the prayer.

Prayer

The prayers included are short and broadly Christian. They are deliberately short in order to help those staff who do not feel comfortable saying prayers. If a member of staff is happy to say prayers they can always extend them themselves.

Follow-up work

A small amount of follow-up work is provided at the end of each group of assemblies so that ideas stimulated in assembly can be followed up in the classroom in greater depth.

A 1. God Knows My Name

You will need:

A doll, pieces of card with numbers on.

Introductory activity

Ask several children to stand up (choose them with care). Give each of them a card with a number on and tell them that they now have a number instead of a name.

Example: Pupil no. 7631007

Ask them if they would like having a number rather than a name. Talk about first names and about choosing names. Ask some members of staff who have children how they went about choosing names for their children. Take a baby doll and ask the children to suggest names for it; decide on one of them. Then talk about surnames. Explain that the family name is usually the name of the father, though this is not always so. As the teacher, you are this baby doll's parent so it will have your surname.

(Note: Some children, e.g. Chinese, may put the surname first.)

Talk

The Bible says that God knows everyone by name. Here are some of the things the Bible says.

Don't be afraid, I have called you by name, you are mine. Just as a mother cannot forget her new-born child so I could never forget you. I have marked your name on the palms of my hand. (Adapted from Isaiah 43:1 and 49:15-16.)

You made every part of me,
I find that difficult to understand!
When I was being made inside my Mum you knew me,
You knew what my life would be like,
You spend your time thinking of me,
I couldn't count the number of times you think of me each day, it
would be like counting the grains of sand on the beach.
I sleep safely because when I awake you are still there.
(Adapted from Psalm 139:13-18)

Comment

It's not very pleasant being a number rather than a name. It makes you feel that people do not really know you. It's even worse when people just point at you and say, 'Here, you!' or 'Thingummy'. Our names mark us out as individuals. Our parents spent time and trouble giving us names.
In the Bible it not only says that God writes our name on his hand, it says he knows all about us. Christians believe that God knows more than our names, he knows the things that make us happy and the things that make us sad. He knows the good things about us and the bad.

Think about it

Think about your name. Say your whole name to yourself silently. If you want to, thank God that he not only knows your name but all about you.

Prayer

Thank you, God, that you know our names and all about us and still love us better than the best parent we can imagine.

A 2. Gifts

You will need:

Some presents – it does not matter what they are, just some items you have been given as presents.

Introductory activity

Ask the children what they would like as birthday presents. Show them some things that you have had for Christmas or birthday.

Ask them what they do with presents once they have got them. Do they play with them, just look at them or put them in a cupboard and forget about them? Make the point that presents are for using, not for hiding away in a cupboard.

Ask one or two of the children to come to the front and roll up their sleeves and show their muscles. Explain that if muscles are not used they get smaller, but if they are used they get bigger.

Story
The parable of the silver coins

Once there was a man who had three servants. One day, when he was going away, he gave one thousand silver coins to one servant, to the next he gave two thousand silver coins and to the third servant he gave five thousand silver coins. The man then went away on his journey.

The servant with five thousand coins used his money and made more money, the servant with two thousand coins did the same, but the servant with one thousand coins took his money, dug a hole in the ground and buried it.

Some time later the man returned and asked his servants what they had done with the money. The servant with five thousand coins told the man what he had done and said, 'Here is your money and here is the extra money I made.' The man was very pleased with him and rewarded him.

The servant with two thousand coins did the same and again the man was very pleased and rewarded him.

The servant with one thousand coins said to the man, 'I hid your money in the ground and here it is.' The man was not very pleased and he took away that servant's money.

Comment

Just as the servants were given money, we were all given some invisible presents when we were born – these are the talents and abilities we have. Christians believe that these talents are given by God and should be used, or, like muscles they will get smaller. Just as a machine gets rusty if it is never used, so our abilities and talents get rusty if they are not used.

The abilities we have are not for boasting about. Christians believe they were given by God for use in helping other people rather than being used for selfish ends, and one day we will have to account for the way we have used what God has given us.

Think about it

Think about the things you are good at. Now think about the things that you are not so good at. Each of us has gifts we can say thank you for.

Prayer

Help us to use the talents you have given us and not let them go to waste. May we use them for you and for others and not for selfish ends.

A 3. Belonging

You will need:

Objects that can be identified as belonging to someone (e.g. books and bags with names in, items of clothing with name tabs on), luggage labels, a sticky label, a Brownie or Cub hat or scarf, the lost property box.

Introductory activity

Hold up some items from the lost property box and try to find out whom they belong to.

We label things to show they belong to us. We put labels on suitcases, clothes and shoes.

Place named objects on the table and ask the children to return them to their owners or say whom they belong to.

We label objects, but not people. People don't wear labels unless they are on a school trip.

Write the school's name on a sticky label and stick it on a child's jumper to show what school they belong to.

How do we know that people belong to a particular school?

How do we know if people are in Cubs or Brownies?
We know the families and friends we belong to – we don't need to wear labels. We belong to the people who love and care for us.

Talk

This is what the Bible says about belonging.

'Don't be afraid for I have made you, I have called you by your name and you belong to me. I will be with you when things go wrong. Life will not get the better of you. You are extra special to me because I love you.'

'Listen, children, I have loved and looked after you since before you were born. I will still love and look after you as you grow older. I will love you even when you are old and grey, for my love for you will never end.'

(Adapted from Isaiah: 46:3 – 4, 43:1 – 2a)

Comment

Christians believe that all people belong to God even if they do not wear labels saying so. They believe that God made the world and the people in it and he cares for them. If Christians could put labels on people they would read like this:
VALUABLE, HANDLE WITH CARE – THIS PERSON BELONGS TO GOD.

Think about it

Think of the people who love and care for you, whether they are your parents, your friends, a foster parent or a relation. People belong where they are loved.

Prayer

Thank you, God, for the people who love and care for us. Thank you for our families and friends. Thank you for your care and love. Help us to remember that we belong to you.

A 4. Value

You will need:

Items worth different amounts (e.g. crisps, a chocolate bar).
Something rare or unique.
A piece of jewellery.
Something made with love and care.
Something of sentimental value.
An old teddy or a comfort rag.

Introductory activity

Hold up a number of objects and ask the children to guess the price, using as a model the television game 'The price is right'. This entails the children guessing what something costs, while the teacher guides them by saying, 'Up a bit', 'Down a bit.'

Include some cheap things, some expensive ones, some with rarity value, some with 'sentimental value' and some made with love and care. The aim is to explore the idea that cost and value are not the same thing, and that value depends on many different things.

Go through the objects a second time and ask the children to state their *value*, in terms of 'not much', 'a lot', etc.

Talk

Some things, such as a gold ring, are valuable because they are made of expensive materials. Some things, such as a painting, are valuable because they are unique (the only one). Some things are valuable because of whom they belonged to, who gave them or who made them. Some things are valuable because they are loved, like an old teddy. Some things are valuable because they have been made with loving care.

Jesus said this about the value of people: 'If God cares about every sparrow that falls, how much more does he care about people! If God takes the trouble to make wild flowers beautiful, how much more does he care for humans.'

Comment

Christians believe that people are so valuable that no one could ever buy a person. They are valuable not because they are made of silver or gold like a ring but because they are made by God. People are precious because God makes every person different, even identical twins. Each person is like a unique piece of art.

Most important of all, he makes them with love and care, as parents might make a toy for a child. For a Christian every human is valuable because of who made them; it is like being a painting signed by a famous artist – God. Just as you treat a valuable object with love and care, so people, made by God, should be treated with love and care, not because they always behave as if they deserve it but because of who made them.

Think about it

Think about valuable things such as diamonds, paintings, precious objects. Some things are called 'priceless' – they are so valuable that no one could think of a price to put on them. You are more valuable than any object. Each person is priceless.

Prayer

May we always treat each other as valuable because of the love and care you give to each person.

A 5. Everyone Is Needed

You will need:

A large sheet of paper with drawings of an ear, an eye, a hand and a foot.

Introductory activity

Talk about these parts of the body and how we need them. Talk about the job that each one does. Demonstrate this by doing the following:
 (a) Play a short game of 'I Spy'.
 (b) Ask a child to hop or skip (not with a rope).
 (c) Ask the children to pick up various objects with their hands.
 (d) Ask them to listen to different sounds and guess what they are.

Talk

We need each part of our body, yet each part is different. Here is what the Bible says:
The body is not made up of one part but of many. The foot cannot say, 'Because I am not a hand I am not a part of the body.' Neither can the ear say, 'Because I am not an eye I am not a part of the body.' If the whole body were an eye how would we hear? If the whole body were an ear how would we smell things? The eye cannot say to the hand, 'I don't need you.' Neither can the head say to the feet 'I don't need you.' Each part of the body is needed. God has made the body so that there are many different parts and each part needs the others. Only together do they make a whole body.
(I Corinthians 12:14-27)

Comment

Different people are a bit like the parts of a body. Each part is different, each has its own job to do. The foot isn't useless because it can't sing, neither is the eye useless because it can't run. Christians believe that God makes us all different, but each person has their own gifts which they can use for others. Each person is different and each person is needed.

Think about it

Think of the things you can do. How can you use those gifts for others?

Prayer

Thank you, Father, for the gifts you have given us. Teach us to use them wisely and unselfishly.

Follow-Up Work for the Classroom

1. The children can draw portraits of each other and write down each other's special gifts.
2. In the Good News Bible, look at the extract from Psalm 139 used in the assembly A1. Ask the children to put it in their own words – this could be spoken or written work.

B 1. Commitment

You will need:

A ball of string; pen and paper (optional).

Introductory activity

Begin by saying that you cannot tell just by looking at people that they are friends, so you are going to link them together so that everyone knows.

Choose someone you know to have some friends there and ask her to come out to the front. This person holds the ball of string and calls out the name of a friend. The friend comes out to the front and the first person passes the ball of string to him, keeping hold of the end. The second person repeats this passing the ball to his friend and keeping hold of the string. Repeat this until you have a 'web' of friendship. (Use no more than half the number of children present, so that there is not a small number 'left out'.)

Talk about the invisible ties that bind people to their friends and the people they love. Those 'ties' are *love, loyalty, commitment* and *caring*. If you wish, write these words on paper and attach them to the 'web'. Explain that people stay with their friends not because they have to, as they would if they were really tied to them, but because they are tied by invisible strings of friendship.

Story

Here is a story about a girl called Ruth and how she chose to be tied by love and loyalty to her new family.

Naomi and her husband had two sons. One son was married to Ruth and one was married to Orpah. Naomi's home was in Bethlehem, but the family did not live there, they lived in another country, called Moab. One day Naomi's husband died and then her two sons died and the three women were left on their own. Orpah went back to her family, but Ruth refused to leave her mother-in-law, Naomi.

Naomi told Ruth to go back to her family where life would be comfortable, for she had nothing to offer Ruth but a life of hardship and poverty.

Ruth said to Naomi, 'Don't ask me to leave you or to stop following you, for where you go, I will go. Where you live, I will live. Your people shall by my people. Your God shall be my God. Where you die, I will die and there I will be buried also. I make this promise before God. Nothing but death shall ever separate us.'

Naomi realized that Ruth would not leave, so the old woman and the young one set out for Naomi's home town of Bethlehem.

As soon as they got to Bethlehem Ruth started work. She was young and strong and went to work in the fields as a gleaner, picking up the corn others had dropped. People admired her for her love of Naomi and because she was willing to give her time and effort to gather food for them both when she could have had an easy life.

Boaz, the farmer, saw what Ruth was doing. One day he stopped Ruth in the fields and said to her, 'I have heard how you left your home and came here to a strange land to work in the fields and take care of Naomi. God bless you for all you are doing'. Boaz told his workers to 'accidentally-on-purpose' drop some extra grain so that Ruth and Naomi would have plenty for the winter.

Ruth worked hard to support Naomi and eventually she married Boaz the farmer. Ruth and Boaz had children and their grandchild was King David.

Comment

Ruth chose to be tied to Naomi, she did not have to stay with her. We all experience the ties of love and friendship in some way. Christians believe that we can also experience the tie of love and friendship with God.

Think about it

Imagine that a piece of string is tied between you and your friend. In real life there is not a piece of string, but there is an invisible tie called 'friendship'. Think about the invisible things, such as loyalty, which hold you together.

Prayer

Help us, Father, to build those ties of love, loyalty and friendship between ourselves, other people and you.

B 2. *Friends in Need*

You will need:

Paper and pen.

Introductory activity

Tell the children the proverb 'A friend in need is a friend indeed'. Talk about what this means.

Talk about secret messages or signals. Write some secret messages and ask the children to suggest how they can be passed on.

21

Story

This is a story about two friends who had to use a secret signal when they were in danger and one of them was in great need.

David and Jonathan were the best of friends although they led very different lives. David was the son of a farmer and had worked as a shepherd. Jonathan was the son of the king and had been brought up as a prince. As a young boy David had defeated the giant Goliath, when everyone else was afraid of him. After that King Saul sent for David to play music for him whenever he felt in a bad mood. David was a very good soldier, so was Jonathan, but David was the best soldier in the land. Jonathan was not jealous of David; he was pleased when his friend defeated their enemies, but King Saul, Jonathan's father, was very jealous indeed.

Saul thought the people loved David more than they loved him and one day Saul felt so jealous of David that he tried to kill him. David thought he had better go into hiding. Jonathan tried to find out his father's plans so that he could warn David of danger. He arranged a secret signal with his friend. Jonathan would pretend to practise hitting a target with his arrows. If he called out to his servant, 'The arrow is right beside you' then it would be safe for David to return as Saul meant him no harm. If he called out to his servant, 'The arrow is further on' then David would know he had to run for his life.

Jonathan discovered that his father planned to kill David. He could not persuade his father that David was a friend, so he took his servant and went out to the field where David was hiding, pretending to practise his aim with bow and arrow. He shot the arrow deep into the field and called to his servant, 'The arrow is further on'. David knew he had to go, it would be dangerous for Jonathan if they were seen together. Jonathan sent his servant away and said goodbye to David. They hated separating as they had been friends for many years, but for David's sake Jonathan helped him to escape.

Comment

Jonathan remained David's friend even when it became difficult and dangerous. He helped David to escape even though it meant he would not see him again. Jonathan was a friend indeed when his friend David was in need.

Think about it

Think about friendship as you listen to this reading.

When I need you, will you be there?
When I'm in trouble, will you help?
When I'm sad, will you make me laugh?
When I really need you, will you care?

When I cry, will you turn away?
When I make a mistake, will you laugh at me?
When other people tease me, will you join in?
When I really need you, will you care?

Prayer

Help us to remain true to our friends and not let them down when they really need us.

B 3. Fair-weather friends

You will need:

A picture of the sun shining and a picture of a rain cloud (both optional). They can be drawn like weather forecast pictures.

Introductory activity

Explain the term 'Fair-weather friends', using the cloud and sun pictures. Talk about friends who are nice to people when everything is all right (sunny), when they have new toys or sweets or are popular, but ignore their friends when they haven't these things: when life gets a bit stormy they desert their friends.

Story

Once there was a man who had two sons. The youngest son went to his father and told him that he wanted his share of the family money now; he did not want to wait until he was old to get his share of the wealth. Sadly his father let him have the money and at once the son left home and travelled to a far country. Away from home the son set out to enjoy himself, squandering his money on everything he wanted, and he had many friends who helped him spend it.

One day the money ran out and as fast as his money disappeared so did his friends. Food became very scarce in that country and the boy became hungry. Where were his friends now that he was poor and needed them? The boy was so poor that he had to take a job feeding pigs and he was so hungry he ate some of the pigs' food. 'I've been stupid,' he thought, 'I've wasted all my father's money on people who cared nothing about me and now I am hungry and poor. At home even my father's servants eat well. I will go home to my Dad and tell him that I am sorry and that I am no longer fit to be called his son, I'll be a servant instead.'

The son began the long walk home. But when he got there he never really had time to deliver his speech for his father was looking out for him and spotted him when he was still a long way off. The father ran to meet him and flung his arms around him, welcoming him back. 'Bring out good clothes for my son,' he called to his servants, 'and a ring for his finger. Get out the special food and invite everyone to a party, for this is my son whom I thought was lost and I have found again. I thought he was dead but he is alive!'

Comment

The son in this story suffered from fair-weather friends, who deserted him as soon as he had no money. But his father welcomed him back despite all he had done and cared little that the son had wasted his money. Christians believe that God is like the father in this story.

Prayer

Father, teach us to stand by our friends whatever circumstances are like and not to desert them as soon as times are difficult. We are glad that you are not a fair-weather friend; you are always close to us, particularly when times are hard.

B 4. *Friends Who Made an Effort*

You will need:

A sleeping bag.

Introductory activity

Show the sleeping bag to the children and talk about how people sleep when they camp.

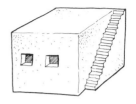

Middle-eastern house

Story

In Jesus's day people used roll-up beds, rather like the ones we use for camping. This is a story about four friends who lifted up a man on his bed and took him to see Jesus.

The man in the story was unable to walk. He was very sad because he had never known what it was like to run or walk, to skip or hop. There were no wheelchairs in those days so the man was stuck in one place and he had to beg for a living as he could not work. Although the man was sad that he could not walk, he was happy because he had four good friends. One day his friends told him they were taking him to see Jesus – they had heard that Jesus could cure people and they wanted their friend to walk. Each friend took a corner of the bed and together they took the man to the house where Jesus was staying. When they got there they were dismayed because the house was so full they could not get in. There were so many people who wanted to see Jesus that they were spilling out of the door into the street. But one of the friends had an idea.

In Israel the houses have outside staircases which lead up to the flat roof. The friends carefully carried their lame friend up to the roof and laid him down. Then they rolled up their sleeves and began to make a hole in the roof. Soon the hole was big enough for them to let the lame man down, using ropes tied to the bed. Jesus was so impressed with the faith of the four friends that he healed the lame man straight away. The man picked up his bed and carried it home himself.

Comment

This man's friends went to great efforts to get him healed. They put themselves out because they cared about him. They didn't mind the journey and the work of making a hole in the roof, their reward was seeing their friend healed and walking.

Think about it

Legs are for running, jumping, skipping and dancing.
Legs are covered in bruises when we fall over.
Legs are for gym and football, hopscotch and ballet.
Legs are for running to help a friend.
Legs take us where we want to go.
Legs are something to be thankful for.

Prayer

Father, help us to be the sort of people who do not mind working hard for our friends when they need us.

B 5. When Friends Fail

You will need:

Some rope or toy handcuffs.

Introductory activity

Talk with the children about being let down by friends. Then show them the rope or handcuffs and tell them that today's story is about Jesus's arrest.

Story

None of Jesus's friends stood by him when life got difficult. One day Jesus warned his disciples that they would all leave him when he was in danger. Peter protested that he would never leave him, but Jesus told him that before he heard the cock crow, Peter would say three times that he never knew Jesus.

Later on that evening Jesus was arrested and all his friends ran away in case they too were caught. Only Peter tried to stop Jesus being arrested – he took out a sword and chopped off the ear of one of the servants who was with the soldiers. Jesus told Peter off gently; he knew Peter was trying to help, but Jesus was not a violent man. He healed the man's ear and said to Peter, 'Those who live by the sword die by the sword'.

Peter followed the soldiers at a distance so that he could see where they had taken Jesus. When he got near the place where Jesus was being questioned, one of the women there recognized Peter and asked him if he was a friend of Jesus. Peter was frightened. 'No,' he said, 'I never knew the man.' Another servant came up to Peter and she too thought he was one of Jesus's friends. Peter got angry and said, 'I've told you once already, I never knew the man you call Jesus.' Then a man came up to Peter and he too recognized him by his accent. Once again Peter denied ever knowing Jesus and just at that moment a cock crowed twice. Peter started to cry when he remembered what Jesus had said, 'Before the cock crows you will deny three times ever knowing me.'

Comment

This is a sad story about Peter failing as a friend. Of all the disciples Peter was the bravest, but even he failed at the end. Jesus forgave him and Peter became one of Jesus's best friends again. He went around the world telling others about Jesus. Peter became very brave, he faced hardships and dangers and eventually he was killed many years later.

Peter may have failed once but that did not wreck his friendship with Jesus; Jesus forgave him and Peter became an even better friend. That often happens when we make mistakes or fail our friends. We can either let it ruin a friendship or we can be forgiven, learn from our mistakes and the friendship can grow and deepen.

Think about it

Sometimes the most courageous thing we can do is to admit we were wrong. To say you were wrong yesterday means that you are a wiser person today. Think about some of the times you have done things you wish you hadn't. We have all done things we regret, but we can learn from those mistakes. The mistakes can help us to change for the better.

GROUP B: Friends

25

Prayer

Help us to learn from our mistakes and not let them ruin our friendships. Teach us the value of forgiveness and saying sorry.

Follow-up Work for the Classroom

1. Get the children to write a 'job description' for a friend.
2. Write down some of these stories. Leave a large margin and ask the children to decorate the margin with something related to the story, for example, wheat for Ruth, bows and arrows for David and Jonathan. Collect the stories into a folder.

C 1. *Sharing Unselfishly*

$$4 \div 2 \qquad 8 \div 2 \qquad 10 \div 5$$

You will need:

A variety of items to share – some money, some sweets, a cake or some biscuits. A large sheet of paper and felt-tipped pens.

Introductory activity

Do some *very simple* sharing sums with the children.
Example: I have ten sweets and I share them equally with my friend. How many do we get each?

Take one item and share it unfairly with the children, so that you get more than they do. Ask the children what is wrong with this.

Ask the children to share out some of your items fairly. Then ask them to imagine they have only one sweet. If they share it with someone else they will have hardly anything. That is when sharing becomes really difficult.

Story

This is a story about someone who shared their very last meal.

There had been no rain in Israel for some time. God told the prophet Elijah to go to a town called Zarephath. When Elijah arrived at the town gate he met a poor widow collecting sticks for her fire. Elijah said to the woman, 'Please could I have some bread and some water?' The woman replied, 'I have only got a tiny bit of oil and flour left. I am collecting sticks for a fire to cook a last meal for my son and myself.'

'Don't be afraid,' said Elijah. 'Go ahead and make your last meal but would you share it with me? Don't worry, you will not starve for God has said that your oil and flour will be renewed each day until the rains come again.'

The woman trusted Elijah and shared her last meal, and after that each day there was oil and flour in her jar, enough for one day's meals.

Comment

Sharing is easy when it does not really affect you. It is much more difficult when it costs you a lot. Sharing is not only about money or possessions, people can also share their time and their friendship with other people.

Sharing time does not just mean sharing odd moments of time when we haven't got anything else to do – that is easy. Real sharing is when people give up their time to be with others when they would rather be doing something else.

Sharing possessions with others means sharing your best toys, not just the ones you don't want any more.

Think about it

Sharing should be a sharing of the things that really matter to us. Think carefully about that as you listen to this reading.

Not just my left-overs,
Not just my old clothes,
Not just my broken toys,
But my best.

Not just my torn books,
Not just my spare time,
Not just my casual friendship,
But my best.

Prayer

Help us to share even when it costs. Teach us not to hold back our help to those in need.

C 2. Sharing What We Have

You will need:

Items for a picnic.

Introductory activity

Have a picnic ready packed up. Open it and show what is in it.

Ask the children what they have in their packed lunches. You could arrange for one or two children to bring their packed lunch into assembly and show the others.

Tell the story of the feeding of the five thousand, emphasizing the smallness of the boy's lunch.

Story

The Feeding of the Five Thousand

Lots of people followed Jesus to hear him speak. One day a great crowd of about five thousand people followed him to a deserted place. All day the people listened to Jesus, and as it got near evening they began to feel tired and hungry. Jesus felt sorry for them and asked the disciples what food they had with them. The disciples replied that they had no food and they did not have enough money to buy food either.

Andrew, one of Jesus's friends, found a small boy who had brought his packed lunch with him. The boy had five small loaves of bread and two fish, and he gave them to Jesus.

Jesus told the people to sit down on the grass, then he said 'thank you' to God and shared the loaves and the fish between the people. The more bread and fish Jesus gave away, the more there was. Soon everyone had enough to eat and there were even crumbs left over which were collected into baskets.

Comment

The boy probably thought he could do very little to help when everybody was hungry, but Jesus took what he had and used it. Christians believe this is still true – Jesus can take people's talents, time, goods and money and use them. Often people feel they can do very little because the need is so great and they are so small, but Jesus can use whatever we have.

Think about it

When we feel we have little to give – so little that it is no more than a drop in the ocean of need – may we remember that the ocean is after all only a large number of drops.

Prayer

What we have to give often seems very little. Teach us to share and trust in you to use it. A little in your hands can go a long way.

C 3. Sharing Ourselves

You will need:

A clock, some toys and some sweets.

Introductory activity

Show the children the items you have brought in and ask how each of them could be shared. Explain that the clock represents the time we have, if the children do not suggest this themselves.

Story

As Jesus was talking to the crowds, some people brought their children to him. They wanted Jesus to put his hands on the children and bless them. The disciples, however, thought that Jesus was too busy and tired to bother with children, so they would not let the children near him. When Jesus heard about this he was cross. 'Don't stop the children from coming,' he said, 'For God's kingdom is for those people who are like little children. In fact, those who are not like little children will not be able to get in.' Jesus turned to the children and put his arms around them. He placed his hands on their heads and prayed for them.

Comment

Jesus not only shared his time and his possessions with people, he shared himself, even when he was very tired. He was not too busy to bless the children.

Harvest is about sharing; it is a time when people thank God for the goodness of the earth and share the things God has given them. Christians believe that God not only gives people food to share, he gives them time and even themselves to share as well.

Think about it

Sharing isn't always easy. Listen carefully to the reading and think about it.

It's not easy to share my toys,
My books, my clothes, my games.
It's not easy.

It's not easy to share my time,
My friends, my ideas, myself.
It's not easy.

People break toys, tear books,
Spoil clothes, steal friends,
Laugh at my ideas and hurt me.
It's not easy.

Prayer

As we share the food that harvest brings, may we also share our time, our money and ourselves
with others, even though this may be very hard.

C 4. *Thank You*

Introductory activity

Talk to the children about saying 'thank you'. When do people say 'thank
you'? Why do they say 'thank you'? What happens when they don't say it?

Story

In Jesus's time leprosy was a terrible disease which was very common and could not be
cured. Now it can be treated. Leprosy was catching and people who had this disease had to
leave home and live out in the country away from villages and towns. Often they wore a bell
to warn others to keep away from them. Not only was the disease painful, it meant that
sufferers led very lonely lives.

One day Jesus met ten men who had leprosy. He was very sad to see them suffering so
much and separated from their families, so he healed them. The men were so glad to be
cured they ran back to their homes straight away. Only one of them stopped, turned back
and thanked Jesus. All the others were so glad to be cured they forgot to say 'thank you'.

Comment

Jesus healed ten people but only one stopped to say 'thank you'. Saying 'thank you' isn't just
being nice, it is recognizing what someone has done for you. When people cease to say
'thank you' to each other, they just take each other for granted, they don't notice the number
of things the other person does for them. Your parents might complain about being taken for
granted. You may not even notice all the things they do for you. For one day try to keep a
record of all the things your Mum and Dad do for you and say 'thank you' to let them know
you have noticed. Harvest is a time of saying 'thank you' to God. Most of the time people do
not notice what he does for them but harvest acts as a reminder to say 'thank you'.

Think about it

Try to think of some of the things you can silently say 'thank you' for. For example, we do not
think of saying 'thank you' for being healthy until we are ill.

Prayer

Thank you, Father, for all you do that we never notice. Forgive us for the number of times we
fail to say 'thank you'.

C 5. The Unlabelled Present

You will need:

A box wrapped as a present with a few items of food inside.
A large sheet of paper and a pen.

Introductory activity

Ask some children to open the box and see what is inside. Ask them who the present was from. Get them to search the box for a label indicating who sent the present. Explain that if you do not know who sent the present, it makes it difficult to send a thank-you letter.

Talk

Say that you are going to write a thank-you letter for the present and ask the children to help write it. Put a large question mark where the name should be. Explain that it will be difficult to send because you do not have an address.

Comment

Christians think of the world as a large present from God, but it has not got a label on it saying who sent it. If Christians wrote a thank-you letter for the harvest they would cross out the question mark and write God. Let's do this with our letter.
(You could then read out the letter.)

Think about it

Think about one thing that you can say 'thank you' for today. Decide whom you are going to say 'thank you' to and why. It might be the lollipop lady or the caretaker, your parents or a brother or sister.

Prayer

Thank you, God, for the sun and the rain that give us our food. Help us to remember that all we have comes from you.

C 6. Corn Dollies

You will need:

A corn dolly (optional),
Three art straws, some coloured ribbon, some white wool or cotton, scissors.

Introductory activity

Show the children the corn dolly if you have one and explain how they are made.

Tie the three straws together at the top. Plait the length of the straws leaving about 6 inches unplaited at the end. Loop the plait. Tie the ribbon to hold the loop. Trim the protruding straws diagonally.

Talk

This is a very simple corn dolly. The real ones are more complicated and are made from straw. The word 'dolly' comes from the word 'idol' and originally these dollies were made in the shape of a goddess of grain who was worshipped in the hope that she would make the crops grow. People thought they had to worship the goddess to make her produce crops each year; if there was a bad harvest they thought they had made her angry.

When people became Christians this custom ceased to be a way of persuading the goddess to produce good crops. Christians believe that God does not need persuading to send the rain and the sun which the crops need. He has already promised that he will send cold and heat, day and night, summer and winter. But that does not mean there will never be a bad harvest. Often people ill treat the land and it fails to produce a good harvest. Trees are cut down and the soil gets washed away. On other occasions rain comes at the wrong time or not at all and the harvest is poor in some places. But God has made the world so that there is enough food for everyone – if it is shared.

Corn dollies are still used, usually for decoration rather than anything else. The corn dolly could now be used as a reminder that God keeps his promises.

Think about it

Think about hot weather and playing in the sun.
Think about cold weather and making snowmen.
Think about the rain and splashing in puddles.

Prayer

Thank you, Father, that you keep your promises and that day and night, heat and cold, summer and winter, never fail.

C 7. News Flash

You will need:

A desk and a chair.

Talk

Sit at a desk and pretend to read the local news bulletin. Halfway through give out a news flash.

'I have just received a news flash from the local Electricity Board. Owing to a fault at one of the power stations, electricity supplies will be cut immediately for an indefinite period. Power will be cut to all homes and business premises; only hospitals and the emergency services will continue to receive electricity.

Explain that your news was fictitious but ask the children what life would be like if this really happened. What would they miss most – the television, lights, electric cookers? Ask the children for suggestions.

Comment

We all depend very heavily on each other. Often we do not notice how much we depend on other people, like the people who work in the power stations or the coalmines until there is an emergency like this. If people stop working for any reason, we realize how much we depend on each other. Christians believe that we also depend on God who never stops working.

Think about it

We all depend on a lot of other people we do not know. Listen carefully to this reading.

I do not know your name, but thank you.
Thank you for my water,
And the power that heats it.
Thank you for my food,
And the gas that cooks it.
I do not know your name, but thank you.

Thank you for the bus that takes me to school,
And the factory which made it.
Thank you for the food I eat,
And the workers who grew it.
I do not know your name, but thank you.

Thank you for the clothes I wear,
And the people who made them.
Thank you for the books I read,
And the people who wrote them.
I do not know your name, but thank you.

Prayer

Thank you for all the people we depend on who make our lives richer by their work. Thank you that we can depend on you and you will never let us down.

C 8. Promises

You will need:

Enough thick felt-tip pens to make a rainbow. (Alternatively, use wax crayons sideways.) A large sheet of paper.

Introductory activity

Talk about the promises people make. Why do people sometimes break their promises? (They forget, don't bother, deliberately break them or find that keeping them is out of their control.)

Draw a rainbow, asking the children to tell you all the colours. Talk about when a rainbow can be seen.

Talk

You have probably all heard the story of Noah's ark and how he rescued the animals from the flood. After the waters had gone down God said to Noah that never again would the earth be flooded in that way and he put a rainbow in the sky as a sign of that promise. He also said that there would be seedtime and harvest, heat and cold, summer and winter, day and night. Christians believe that it is because of this promise that our crops can grow and we have harvest festival. Without heat and cold, day and night, and the seasons, our food would not grow. Every time you see a rainbow, remember that the Bible says it is a sign of God keeping his promise.*

Comment

This promise from God is very important. Without it life could not go on. Christians believe that God keeps his promise because he wants to and he has the power to do so.

Think about it

Think of some of the promises you make. Do you always keep your promise?

Prayer

Thank you for the cold of winter and the heat of summer days. Thank you for the dark nights and the light of the sun. Thank you for keeping your promise.

*You may wish to refer to the talk in **C6** to explain why the harvest sometimes does fail.

C 9. The Harvest of Life

You will need:

Some vegetables and fruit, a mushroom basket, or something similar, a felt-tipped pen, a pair of scissors, some card.

Introductory activity

Talk about harvest time and the different fruits and vegetables that are gathered.

Explain that the harvest is the result of the complete life of the plant or tree. Different plants produce different types of fruit, such as apples, potatoes, nuts. Show your selection of fruit and vegetables and place them in the basket. Say that harvest is simply the end result of a plant's life.

Talk

The Bible talks about the harvest of life. Just as apple trees produce apples and vines produce grapes, so people's lives produce different things. Some people's lives produce love, friendship and peace, but other people produce hatred, war and greed.

'You know a tree by the fruit it produces,' said Jesus.

Place your mushroom basket on the table and ask the children to think carefully about what they will put in their harvest basket of life. Get them to think of the good things that people's lives produce. Write some of the children's suggestions on pieces of card and attach them to the fruit and vegetables.

E.g. apple – joy, orange – love, potato – friends.

Think about it

As we see fruit and vegetables being produced at this time of year, it is a good time to think about the produce of our own lives. Close your eyes and imagine a harvest basket like the one here. Sit and think for a while. What would you really like to produce with your life?

Prayer

Help us, God, to produce good with our lives and to reject all that is wrong and false.

C 10. Reaping and Sowing

You will need:

Seeds, pips, stones and the matching fruit and vegetables.
You can sellotape the seeds to paper so that children can see them easily when you hold them up, or you can place them on an overhead projector slide.

Introductory activity

Ask the children to guess which seed produces which plant. Try to match them all up.

Talk

If a farmer sows carrot seeds he gets carrots, if he sows wheat seeds he gets wheat. You cannot expect to sow potatoes and pick peaches or sow mushrooms and get grapes! What you sow is what you reap or pick.

The Bible says that life is like a farmer who sows seed in a field – what you put into life decides what you get out of it. If you sow hatred you cannot expect to get love. If you sow anger you cannot expect to get peace.

There is no guarantee of this because life is not always fair. Some people sow love, but others may treat them badly even though they do not deserve it. But, generally what you put into life decides what you get back.

Comment

Life is like planting seeds. Imagine a patch of earth and a tiny seed buried underneath it. What 'seeds' do you want to plant? You can plant seeds of love or you can plant seeds of selfishness and hate.

Prayer

Teach us, God, to sow only good in life and help it to grow and multiply.

Follow-up Work for the Classroom

1. Make a harvest collage showing all the different results of people's labour. Use pictures from magazines and brochures, as well as the children's drawings, if you wish.
2. Make a 'thank you' display of all the different things children would like to say 'thank you' for.
3. In art classes the children could make some 'thank you' cards.

D 1. Michaelmas (29 September)

You will need:

An item of clothing with a St Michael label in it.

Introductory activity

Talk about fighting and the types of things people fight about. Ask whether the children know what shop uses the brand name 'St Michael'. Tell them that this assembly is about St Michael.

Talk

Many of us have fights over little things. We argue with friends and brothers and sisters. Sometimes arguments develop into fights.

We know very little about Saint Michael, but in the Christian tradition he is usually shown as an angel fighting the Devil. If you go to Coventry Cathedral you will see a sculpture of Saint Michael standing with the Devil under his feet. On St Michael's day or Michaelmas, Christians remember that good is stronger than evil, that love is stronger than hate. One way in which Christians picture this belief is to draw one of God's angels (Michael) standing on the Devil who has been defeated in the fight. It is rather like a boxer standing with one foot on a defeated opponent and a hand in the air for victory.

Saint Michael's day is on 29 September. It was a very important day in medieval Britain. On Saint Michael's day rents were paid, workers were employed for the coming year and great fairs were held. These were sometimes called goose fairs or hiring fairs.

Comment

Ask the children whether they know of a local Michaelmas fair; it will be some time between 29 September and 11 October if it is an old goose fair.

Next time you go to the fair remember Saint Michael and what the fairs were originally for.

Think about it

Imagine a fight in a boxing ring and the defeated person on the floor. Then think of it as a picture of Christian belief: good is stronger than evil, love is stronger than hate.

Prayer

Thank you, Father, for the story of Saint Michael to remind us that evil is a defeated power.

D 2. One World Week (end of October)

You will need:

Various items of food that come from other parts of the world.

Introductory activity

Show the children the items of food that come from different countries. Look at the wrappers on the various foods and find out where they come from. Use a world map if you wish.

Talk

We depend on many countries for our food and our clothing. Without the produce of other countries our diet would be much more limited. There would be no oranges or bananas, no coffee or chocolate. Our cotton clothes come from India and the Middle East, the leather for our shoes is not all produced in this country. We need to buy things from other countries, just as they need things from us. What happens in any part of the world affects us all. A disaster in one part of the world is a disaster for us all because we are all connected. We all depend on each other.

Comment

The world is like a giant family – each part is related to the others. Each part needs the others. Some parts of the family are rich, some parts are poor. Some are healthy and some are sick. Within families people help each other. One world week is a time when people remember this giant family and try to help each other, to make the world a better place.

Think about it

How many people are there in your own family? Try to imagine a family with millions of people.

Prayer

Thank you, Father, for the giant family of the human race. Thank you for the world you have given us – its hot deserts and cold ice and snow. May we look after this world you have created and make it a fairer world for all.

D 3. All Hallows' Eve

You will need:

A large calendar.

Introductory activity

Ask the children what month it is and what day. Ask one child to find the right place on the calendar. Ask the children to find tomorrow's date and next month. Ask them when the new year starts. If you wish to, talk a little about Hallowe'en, *but with care and sensitivity,* in a way that will reassure children. This assembly is designed to help allay any fears that Hallowe'en might engender in children, it is not an assembly on Hallowe'en. This might be a good time to talk about the safety aspect of 'Trick or Treat' and possibly discourage children from this practice for the sake of their safety and to protect people from vandalism.

Talk

Many years ago the New Year began on 1 November. It was a time when people looked towards the future and wondered what was going to happen, especially through the dark days of winter. Many people were frightened of what might happen in the future, that is one of the reasons why there are many scary customs associated with Hallowe'en. Christians believe the future is nothing to be afraid of because God is always there. Here is what Saint Paul said when he was afraid:

'If God is on our side who can defeat us? ... Who can separate us from the love of Christ? Can trouble or hardship, hunger or poverty, danger or death? No, we can triumph over all these things through the love of Christ! I am sure that nothing can separate us from his love; nothing in life or death, above or below. No ruler or power, present or future will ever be able to separate us from the love of Christ our lord.' (Adapted from Romans 8:31-9)

Comment

Paul faced many frightening situations in his life but he knew that God was always with him, and that God never stopped loving and caring for him. Christians believe that God is always with them, however frightened or uncertain they may be.

Think about it

Think carefully about this reading as you listen to it.

Fear is an icy hand,
My bedroom without the light,
The countryside in the dark.
Being by myself in a strange place.

Security is a warm blanket,
It's turning on the light,
Daylight creeping over the fields,
Knowing you are always there.

Prayer

When we are frightened help us to remember that you are there and always loving us.

D 4. All Saints' or All Hallows' Day (1 November)

You will need:

Paper, pen and Blu-Tak.

Introductory activity

Draw a matchstick person and put a halo on the figure. Explain that the word 'halo' comes from the word hallowed which means saintly or good. Originally the word 'saint' just meant a Christian, but now it is used to describe a special sort of Christian.

Ask the children if they know the names of any local churches, schools, buildings or streets which are named after saints.

Talk

Some special Christians are called saints. In pictures they are sometimes drawn with a halo round their head. It is not there in real life, it is just a sign or symbol that artists use to represent goodness. On All Saints' Day all the saints are remembered. Many people are named after saints. How many of you have saints' names? Here are a few names: put your hand up if you hear your name or one that is very like it.

Catherine, John, Mark, Martin, Christina, Joan, Adrian, Angela, Antony, Christopher, Theresa, Bernadette, Charles, Damian, Helena, Daniel, David, Margaret, Ann, Paula, Madelaine, Nicholas, Victoria, Elizabeth, Edward, Frances, Joseph, Justin, Lucy, Rose, Mary, Simon, William, Paul, Luke, James, Natalia, Monica, Veronica, Viviana, Stephen.

Comment

All Saints' Day is a celebration of goodness. It is a time when Christians thank God for the lives of those people who have left the world a better place than they found it. Look around your village/town/city, and see if you can find streets, churches or buildings named after saints.

Think about it

Think quietly for a moment about the unknown saints – all the people whose courage and love is untold. Somewhere there is a Saint Fred getting on with the job of loving others. Somewhere there is a Saint Karen standing up for right in the face of danger. All over the world there are the everyday saints spending their lives in the service of God and others.

Prayer

Here is the prayer of a famous saint called Saint Francis.

Lord, make me a bringer of peace.
Where there is hatred let me bring love;
Where there are hurt feelings may I bring forgiveness;
When someone has lost their way to you may I help them find you again.

May I bring hope where there is none;
Light where there is darkness;
Joy where there is sadness.
Lord, may I cheer others up instead of wanting them to cheer me up.
May I understand rather than wanting others to understand me first.
May I love others rather than always wanting them to love me.
For it is in giving ourselves that we receive,
It is in forgetting ourselves that we find out who we really are.
It is in forgiving others that we ourselves are forgiven.

D 5. All Souls' Day (2 November)

You will need:

A tape of a Christmas carol (optional).

Introductory activity

If you feel confident enough, sing a carol (you can do this with a group of children if you wish). If not, talk about carol singing or play a tape of a carol. Explain that people used to sing carols at various festivals, not just at Christmas.

Talk

All Souls' is the day when Christians remember all the people who have died and say 'thank you' for their lives. This used to be a very important festival and people acted out plays and held celebrations. Special cakes called soul-cakes were baked and singers, called 'soulers', went from door to door singing, just like carol singers today, and they were given soul-cakes and other food.*
Here is an old souling carol:
  God bless the master of this house
  And the mistress also,
  And all your little children that round the table grow;
  Likewise your men and maidens,
  Your cattle and your store,
  And all that dwell within your gates
  We wish them ten times more.

  Soul, soul, for a soul cake!
  I pray, good missis, for a soul cake!
  An apple, a pear, a plum or a cherry,
  Any good thing to make us merry.

(Shropshire souling-song)

41

Comment

Although Hallowe'en and All Saints' Day are still remembered, All Souls' Day is not often celebrated now. However, it is a reminder to us to say 'thank you' for the lives of people who have died, for good and brave men and women who were loved by their friends and families.

Think about it

Listen carefully to this reading:

For all the people who changed our world for the better,
We thank you.
For all the people who left behind them new ideas, caring communities, peaceful countries,
We thank you.

Prayer

Thank you, Father, for the lives of those who have died. Thank you for their love and kindness which made a difference to the world we live in.

*A recipe for soul-cakes can be found in *Soul Cakes and Shish Kebabs*, published by RMEP.

Follow-up Work for the Classroom

1. Make a list of all the churches, streets and buildings in your area named Saint Michael's, All Souls' or All Saints'. (You may need to look in the telephone directory for some of them.)
2. If there are any local churches called by these names, find out if there are any windows, banners, paintings or sculptures that you could look at and arrange to make a visit. This may enable the children to find out more about these special days.

E 1. Ideal Friends

You will need:

A large sheet of paper, a pen, Blu-Tak.

Introductory activity

Draw a large matchstick person. Ask the children to tell you qualities they would look for in a friend if they could choose anyone in the world.

Write their suggestions around the matchstick person, to produce the 'perfect friend'. Example:

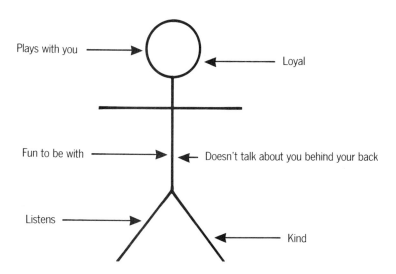

Plays with you

Loyal

Fun to be with

Doesn't talk about you behind your back

Listens

Kind

Talk

We cannot choose any friend in the world. We make friends with the people we meet and we know they are not perfect; neither are we a perfect friend to them. For the next few weeks we shall be looking at how Jesus chose his friends and what those friends were like. Jesus's friends are often called by a special name – they are called his disciples.

Think about it

Think about the type of friend you are to other people. Think about your friends. Are you a good friend to them? Are there ways in which you are not a good friend? How could you improve?

Prayer

Thank you, God, for our friends. May we forgive the mistakes they make, as they forgive us.

E 2. Choosing

You will need:

Some items to choose from: clothes, books, food, holiday brochures, etc. (two or more of each).

Introductory activity

Ask several children to make choices.
For example: 'If you could choose between this jacket and that one which would you choose?'
Ask them to tell you why they made that choice.
Repeat this with other items, always asking a reason for the choice.

Talk

Choosing is sometimes hard. It can be difficult to make up your mind. Some of the choices we make in life are very important.

When Jesus chose his friends he realized it was going to be a very important decision, so he got up very early and talked to God about it. After he had talked with God he started to choose his friends. Jesus could have chosen anybody but he did not choose just intelligent people, or just rich people, or just important people. He did not choose all poor people either; his friends were a very mixed bunch. One had a hot temper, one was hated by other people, one was quite wealthy, others were poor. Each one was different.

Think about it

Think about the different friends you have. Are they all alike? Try to see a picture of them in your mind. Say a silent 'thank you' for each of them.

Prayer

We thank you, Father, for all our friends. We are glad that Jesus chose many different people as his disciples and he still chooses all types of people to be his friends.

E 3. Friends Wanted

You will need:

A large sheet of paper: on it draw a 'wanted poster' with a face sketched in.
Write: WANTED – FRIENDS. REWARD PAYABLE.

Introductory activity

Show the poster and talk about what a 'wanted poster' is normally used for.

Talk about rewards and what sort of things they might be.

**WANTED
FRIENDS**

REWARD PAYABLE

Talk

Not everyone wanted to be Jesus's friend. Some people did not like him because he helped poor and diseased people. Some people did not want to be his friend because he lived a hard life – he had no house, and no money and his work was very hard.

Once when someone asked to be his friend, he said to them, 'The foxes have holes and the birds of the air have nests but I have nowhere to lay my head.' Jesus wanted to make sure that the person had really thought over what it meant to be his friend.

If Jesus had advertised for friends his advertisement might have looked like this:

Wanted, friends, must be used to living a hard life, often sleeping in the open and travelling by foot. Must not mind mixing with the poor, the sick and the outcast. Must be brave because the rulers do not like my work.

Do you think many people would have applied?

Comment

Many people did follow Jesus. Men and women gave up comfortable lives and good jobs to do this. During the next two weeks we are going to look at twelve of Jesus's close friends called disciples. Their reward was not money but friendship with God.

Think about it

Think about those times when it is difficult for you to remain someone's friend – times when other people make fun of them and maybe of you too if you remain their friend. Think about the friends of Jesus and how hard it must sometimes have been for them.

Prayer

Thank you, Father, for those early friends of Jesus who gave up everything to be with him.

E 4. James, Son of Zebedee

You will need:

Paper, pens (scissors, Blu-Tak).

For this series you can draw round children's hands on a large sheet of paper and create a 'Hands of Friendship' display, writing a different disciple's name and nickname on each pair of hands. Alternatively, you could cut out the paper hands and Blu-Tak them to the wall.

Introductory activity

Ask whether any of the children are called James or the feminine equivalent, which is Jackie or Jacqueline. Choose one of them and draw round their hands. Write James, on one hand. Tell them that James means the heel of your foot.

Talk

James was a fisherman, he worked with his father and his brother John, fishing in Lake Galilee. One day Jesus walked along the shore of the lake, he saw James and his brother at work and he called them to follow him. The brothers had met Jesus before; they trusted him enough to leave their nets and follow him. Fishing is a hard job but they knew the life they were about to start would be even harder. James was a good friend to Jesus but he did have a temper! Jesus nicknamed James and John 'Sons of Thunder' because they both had quick tempers.

James was to spend the rest of his life spreading the message of God's love. We also know that James was very brave – in the end he died for his faith.

Write James's nickname, 'Son of Thunder', on the other hand.

Think about it

Think of something that is very precious to you. If someone asked you to give it up, would you do it? What would someone have to offer you to make you give it up? Think about the things James and John gave up to follow Jesus.

Prayer

Thank you, Father, for the example of James who was prepared to give up a good job and comfortable life to follow Jesus.

E 5. John, Son of Zebedee

You will need:

Paper, pens (scissors, Blu-Tak).

Introductory activity

Find out how many children are called John (or Sean, Ian, Ivor, Ivan) or one of its feminine equivalents – Jane, Jeanette, Janice, Joanne, Joanna, Hannah, Anna, Ann or any name with Ann in it. All these names have the same meaning in Hebrew, which is 'God has Favoured'.

Draw around a child's hands and write the name John in one.

Talk

John, like his brother James, was a fisherman and he also had a quick temper. John was very close to Jesus; he was one of a group of three disciples who were Jesus's closest friends. The three were Peter, James and John. When Jesus knew he was going to die he wanted to make sure that his mother Mary would be well looked after. It was John who was asked to look after Mary as if she were his own mother. John must have been a very close friend indeed if Jesus felt he could leave his mother safely in John's care.

Write 'The special friend' on the other hand.

Think about it

Think about your best friend. Think about the things you do together. Think about Jesus's best friend, John, and the sort of things they might have shared together.

Prayer

Thank you for our best friends and all they mean to us. Thank you for the example of John, who looked after Mary when Jesus could no longer take care of her.

E 6. Simon Peter

SIMON PETER

THE ROCK

You will need:

Paper, pens (scissors, Blu-Tak).
A rock or stone.

Introductory activity

Ask how many Peters or Simons there are, or the feminine equivalent – Petra, Simone or Rochelle (little rock). Draw around a child's hands and write the name Simon Peter in one.

Show them the rock and explain that in Greek the word 'rock' is 'petros', from which we get the name Peter. Originally this disciple's name was just Simon, which means 'obedient', but Jesus changed his name to Peter, which means 'rock'.

Talk

Simon was a fisherman, and so was his brother Andrew. When Jesus and Simon met, Jesus recognized Simon's enormous strength, not only his strength of body but his strong character. Jesus called Simon to be his friend, but he changed his name to Peter, which means 'rock', because he could see that Peter's friendship would become as firm as a rock. Jesus was right – only once did Peter fail him, which is another story. Peter went on to become one of Jesus's firmest friends.

Peter was not perfect, he tended to rush into things, acting first and thinking afterwards. It took many years before Peter became as strong as a rock, but Jesus saw at the very first meeting the sort of friend Simon Peter could become.

Write 'the rock' on the other hand.

Think about it

Think about Peter and how firm a friend he was. Think about the times when your friends have stood by you even when it has been hard for them.

Prayer

Father, teach us to stand by our friends and to be a rock, like Peter, that other people can depend on.

E 7. Andrew

You will need:

Paper, pens (scissors, Blu-Tak).

Introductory activity

Ask whether any children are called Andrew or its feminine equivalent, Andrea. Draw around a child's hands and write the name Andrew in one.

Talk

Andrew was Peter's brother. He was already a friend of Jesus and he made sure that his brother met Jesus as well. Andrew was the practical one of the disciples – he always seemed to know what to do. When the crowd of 5000 people were hungry it was Andrew who brought the boy with the five loaves and two fish to see Jesus.

When Jesus first called Andrew and Peter to be his friends he told them that they would have a different job from catching fish. They would become 'fishers of men'. Just as the fisherman draws fish into his net, so Peter and Andrew would draw people into God's family. We do not know what finally happened to Andrew; we only know that he travelled about telling people about Jesus. He is the patron saint of Scotland and his flag is dark blue with a white diagonal cross. If you look closely you can see it in the Union Jack.

Write 'fisher of men' in the other hand.

Think about it

Think about your friends and the practical ways in which you can show them you are their friend. Think about things you can do for them.

Prayer

Help us to be practical in our friendship, like Andrew, telling others about you and spreading the word about God's love.

E 8. Philip

You will need:

Paper, pens (scissors, Blu-Tak).

Introductory activity

Ask how many children are called Philip, or the feminine equivalent, Philippa. The name means 'lover of horses'. Draw around a child's hands and write the name Philip inside.

Talk

Philip lived in the same town as Peter and Andrew. After he had met Jesus, he tried to persuade his friend Nathanael to meet Jesus as well. Nathanael was very reluctant, but Philip insisted that his friend went to see Jesus for himself. 'Come and see,' he said.

Your parents might say something similar to you if you are reluctant to do something. For example, you might not want to try some new food and they might say that you can't possibly know whether you like it or not until you have tried it. They probably ask you to try a little bit of the food first to see if you like it. Christians still believe that it is very difficult to explain what it is like to be a friend of Jesus. It is something that people have to experience for themselves, as Philip did, but it is very difficult to put into words.

Philip's nickname could be 'Come and see'. Write this in the other hand.

Think about it

Think about people you did not like at first but as you got to know them you liked them more.

Prayer

Thank you, Father, for the example of Philip who helped his friend to become a friend of Jesus. Help us not to judge by first impressions, but to get to know people before we make a judgement.

E 9. Nathanael

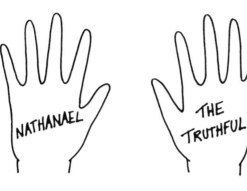

You will need:

Paper, pens (scissors, Blu-Tak).

Introductory activity

Ask whether any children are called Nathanael, Nathan, or Dorothy, which has the same meaning ('gift of God'). Draw around a child's hands and write the name Nathanael inside.

Talk

Nathanael became a friend of Jesus because he had a friend who already knew Jesus. One day his friend told him he must come and meet Jesus for himself. Nathanael was not very keen, 'Can anything good come out of Nazareth?' he said. Nathanael knew that Jesus came from Nazareth and he looked down on the town, because it was not very important. Because of this he nearly missed his chance to become a friend of Jesus. Reluctantly Nathanael met Jesus and at once his attitude changed. Jesus did not tell him off about his prejudice – that he had refused to believe that any good person could come from Nazareth. Instead Jesus commented on Nathanael's good points. 'Here is a man,' said Jesus, 'In whom there is no dishonesty!' Nathanael was 'Nathanael the truthful'. He became one of Jesus's faithful friends.

Write 'the truthful' in the second hand.

Think about it

Think about those times when you have not told the truth. Silently say sorry to God, if you wish.

Prayer

Help us not to be prejudiced against people because of where they come from. Like Nathanael, may we be known as 'the truthful'.

E 10. Thomas

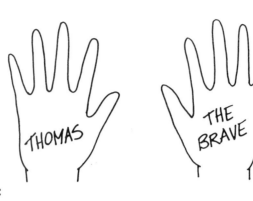

You will need:

Paper, pens (scissors, Blu-Tak).

Introductory activity

Ask whether any children are called Thomas, or the feminine equivalent, Tomasin or Tammie. Draw around a child's hands and write the name Thomas inside.

Talk

Thomas had a twin; we don't know whether he had a twin brother or sister or whether his twin was also a friend of Jesus. Thomas is often called 'Doubting Thomas' because when Jesus rose from the dead Thomas refused to believe that the others had seen him unless he could touch Jesus himself and see the scars on his body. Thomas did see Jesus and he stopped doubting, but the nickname 'Doubting Thomas' has always stuck.

There is another story about Thomas in the Bible which people often forget. Once Jesus was about to go into a very dangerous situation. Everyone was afraid but Thomas said, 'Let's go with Jesus, at least we will die together.' When all the others were afraid Thomas was prepared to die for his friend. Maybe his nickname should be changed from 'Doubting Thomas' to 'Thomas the brave'. Let's write his new nickname in the other hand.

Think about it

Think about the nicknames people have. Are there any hurtful nicknames amongst them? If there are, think of a new nickname that would be less hurtful.

Prayer

Help us, Father, not to give people nicknames which are hurtful and untrue. May the names we give them show the best in them and not the worst.

E 11. James, Son of Alphaeus

You will need:

Paper, pens (scissors, Blu-Tak).

Introductory activity

Ask whether any children have the name James, or the feminine equivalent, Jackie. Draw around a child's hands and write the name James inside.

Talk

We know nothing about James except that he was the son of someone called Alphaeus. James was not an unusual name and he has no nickname that might give us a clue to his character, though he may have been called James the Less. Less could mean that he was short or that he was a younger member of the twelve. His name tells us nothing. Apparently he was not a rock like Simon Peter, neither did he have a bad temper like James and John, the sons of Zebedee. He was not nicknamed 'truthful', 'doubter' or 'brave' and we hear of no stories surrounding him. Maybe James was so ordinary that there was nothing unusual about him to make into a nickname.

Perhaps Jesus chose James just because he was ordinary. There was a place among his friends for someone who was nothing special in anybody else's eyes except Jesus's. Christians believe that all people are special to Jesus. No one is just 'ordinary'.

Maybe James's name should be 'James the ordinary'. Let's write it in the other hand.

Think about it

Imagine what it must be like to be a prince or a princess. What would it feel like to be really special?

Prayer

Thank you, Father, that everyone is really special to you, that each person is a son or a daughter of a heavenly king. We are glad that there was room amongst Jesus's friends for ordinary James who was special to you.

E 12. Judas Iscariot

JUDAS

THE TRAITOR

You will need:

Paper, pens (scissors, Blu-Tak).

Introductory activity

Do not ask for people with this name! *Note:* If there are any children called Jude or a derivative of Judas assure them that Judas was a common name and there were many other people called Judas who were good friends to Jesus. One of them wrote the book of Jude in the Bible. It is also thought that Jesus had a brother with this name.

Draw round your own hands for this one.

Talk

Judas was chosen as Jesus's friend, but in the end he let Jesus down. He told Jesus's enemies where to find him so that they could arrest him. Judas was not a mistake; when Jesus chose him he must have seen some good in him. Judas was not the only one who let Jesus down. The other disciples all ran away when Jesus was arrested and Peter denied ever knowing Jesus.

After he had betrayed Jesus, Judas was so ashamed of himself that he never asked to be forgiven. Because Judas never forgave himself and did not ask for forgiveness he just felt more and more sad and guilty. Peter had also failed Jesus, but he asked Jesus to forgive him and he eventually forgave himself and became one of Jesus's best friends again.

Judas is known as 'Judas the traitor'. He could have had another name, 'Judas the forgiven', if he had asked for help because Jesus said that nothing was unforgivable to God and when he was dying he asked God to forgive the people who had hurt him.

Write 'the traitor' in the other hand.

Think about it

Think about those times when you find it hard to forgive yourself for something you have done. Remember God is always ready to forgive.

Prayer

Saying sorry and asking for forgiveness is hard. Help us to ask for forgiveness and accept it when offered, as you are always willing to forgive us.

E 13. Simon the Zealot

You will need:

Paper, pens (scissors, Blu-Tak).

Introductory activity

Ask which children are called Simon, or the feminine equivalent, Simone, or any other name that shares the same meaning ('obedient').
Draw around a child's hands and write the name Simon inside.

Talk

Simon was probably a fighter. He may have belonged to a group called the Zealots. The whole of this region was occupied by the Romans, the hated enemies. But in Galilee a group called the Zealots were fighting against the Romans. Jesus showed Simon a different way to treat the enemy than fighting them.

The Jews were waiting for a special king to come who would defeat their enemies. Many were expecting a soldier king. Simon was one of those who was waiting for a warrior to come and set his people free. Christians believe that Jesus was that special king, but he was not a soldier. Instead of defeating the enemy, Jesus showed Simon how to love the enemy. In the place of hatred, Jesus preached love. Many had tried to defeat the Romans by war and had failed. Christianity spread through the Roman empire very rapidly, but it did not spread by warfare but by its message of love and forgiveness. Love succeeded in conquering where war had failed.

Write 'the fighter' in the other hand.

Think about it

Think about people who have hurt you or with whom you are no longer friends. Forgiving people is hard but it is better than fighting them. Forgiveness begins with small things. Think of one action you could do or one thing you could say that would show that you wanted to be friends again. Remember that forgiveness also means changing so that you do not hurt one another again.

Prayer

Teach us to love even those we do not like. May we learn a peaceful way of change as Simon the Zealot did.

E 14. Matthew

MATTHEW

THE HATED
THE FRIEND

You will need:

Paper, pens (scissors, Blu-Tak).

Introductory activity

Ask which children are called Matthew, which means 'Gift of the Lord'. Also mention the feminine equivalent, which is Dorothy ('gift of God'). Draw around a child's hands and write the name Matthew inside.

Talk

Matthew was very unpopular because he collected taxes. Tax is the money adults give to the government to pay for the running of the country. Tax collectors were very unpopular in those days because they sometimes increased the taxes people had to pay and kept some money for themselves. The people hated paying tax, not only because it made them poor, but because it went to the hated Roman government. It was bad enough being ruled by the Romans without having to pay for them as well.

One day Jesus saw Matthew collecting taxes and he called him to leave his job and become his friend. Jesus even went to Matthew's house for a meal. Many people were disgusted that Jesus could want a tax collector for a friend but Jesus could see something in Matthew that no one else could. Matthew gave up a rich lifestyle for poverty and hard work as Jesus's friend. When others hated him, only Jesus could see that Matthew could change and follow him.

Matthew had two names. To most people he would have been 'Matthew the hated', but to Jesus he was 'Matthew the friend'. Let's write both these nicknames in the hand.

Think about it

Try to imagine what life was like for Matthew. Imagine no one liking you, no one ever visiting your house and no one saying 'hello' as you walked by.

Prayer

Thank you, Father, that you often see the good in us that no one else sees. When others hated Matthew you loved him.

E 15. Thaddaeus

You will need:

Paper, pens (scissors, Blu-Tak).

Introductory activity

This name means 'loyal, warm and devoted'. The nearest equivalents are Gareth, Garth and Gary, which mean 'gentle'. There is no direct female equivalent, but Naomi means 'pleasant' which is similar. Draw around a child's hands and write the name Thaddaeus inside.

Talk

The name Thaddaeus means 'warm, devoted and loyal'. Not all Jesus's friends were strong fishermen, Thaddaeus may have lived up to his name by being a gentle and loyal companion. We all have different personalities, so Jesus chose friends with very different characters. Maybe Jesus needed a quieter friend as he had James and John 'the sons of thunder' and Peter who was always speaking or doing before he thought about the consequences of his actions.

Thaddaeus's nickname could have been 'Thaddaeus the gentle' or 'Thaddaeus the loyal'.

Write one or both of these in the other hand.

Think about it

Think about the sort of person you are. Are there times when you need to be more gentle with other people?

Activity

At this stage you can look at the display of hands of all the different disciples and their names and nicknames. You might like to ask the children to read out the different nicknames. Talk about the different types of people they were. Say that Jesus chose them all and he chose them with much thought and prayer. He did not choose perfect friends, he accepted their faults, and his friends changed the more they got to know him.

Prayer

Thank you, Father, for each of the disciples – the noisy ones and the quiet ones, the well-known ones and the ordinary ones. Thank you that anyone can be Jesus's friend today.

Follow-up Work for the Classroom

1. Creative writing on friendship, using the ideas in these assemblies.
2. An acrostic poem on the word 'disciple' could be done jointly by the class.
3. The children can make their own wanted posters for friends.

F 1. Communication 1

You will need:

Pen, paper, toy telephone, any other means of communication you can find.

Introductory activity

Talk with the children about communication. Try to list all the different ways people can communicate. For example:

Radio
Television
Spoken word
Telephone
Writing

Talk

Prayer is about communication with God. It needs no equipment, no special language; it can take place at any time and the line is never blocked.

Here are some words from the Bible about God listening to our prayers:

'God is always watching over us and listening to our cries for help.'

'We can trust God at all times and tell him all our troubles for he is like a safe hiding place that we can run to when we are upset.'

'God is ready to answer our prayers before we have even opened our mouths.'

(Selected from the Psalms and Isaiah)

Comment

Christians believe they can pray in any place at any time and God will listen and act. They believe that he is never too busy to listen to anybody, whether it is the most important person in the land or the smallest child.

Think about it

How easy do you find it to listen to others or are you always doing the talking? Think quietly for a moment and during the day try to make a special effort to listen to others.

Prayer

Thank you, Father, that you always listen to us and are concerned about every part of our lives.

F 2. Communication 2

You will need:

A letter, a 'thank-you' card, a notelet with an apology, a list of things you need.

Introductory activity

Talk about sending messages from one person to another. Discuss all the different kinds of messages you can send.

Go through the different items you have and read out part of each one.

Talk

Prayer can be many things. It can be telling God how good he is, like a letter to a friend where you say nice things about them. It can be saying sorry. It can be saying 'thank you' like a 'thank-you' note.

Prayer can also be asking for others or yourself, a bit like a list of things you really need. But prayer is not a shopping list. When you pray for things you need, it is about the real needs of life, such as health and friends, not a list that reads like a letter to Santa.

Prayer can also be telling God how we feel, as we might do in a letter to a close friend.

Christians believe that prayer is many things, and asking is only one small part.

Think about it

If you pray, think about what you usually say to God. Are you always asking for things or do you say other things as well?

Prayer

Thank you, Father, that we can say many different things to you. Help us to remember that and not just ask you for things.

F 3. Praise 1

You will need:

Some work with good comments on it.
Paper and pens.

Well done! Good work!

Much better

Introductory activity

Read out the comments on the pupils' work.

Explain that good comments are called praise – praise means saying something good about someone. Ask the children to suggest words of praise that might be put on the bottom of work. Write them down.

Talk

Here are some words about praise from the Bible.

Let's praise God with the sound of a trumpet.
Tell everyone how good he is with the twang of a guitar.
Let's praise God by dancing to the tambourine,
Shout his name to the sound of the drums.
Praise God with violins and recorders,
Let cymbals crash the greatness of the Lord.
Let every living person praise God.

(Adapted from Psalm 150)

Comment

Prayer can also be praise. It can be a way of saying something good about God. Christians praise God when they start their prayers by telling God how great he is. It is like looking at God's work and writing a good comment on it.
What sort of comments do you think Christians might write about God?

(If you wish, write some of the comments on the paper.)

Think about it

Think about how you feel when someone says something nice to you. Think about those times when you have said something good to someone else.

Prayer

Thank you, Father, for all you do for us that we never realize, all the daily things that go unnoticed.

F 4. Praise 2

You will need:

Some paper and a pen (optional).

Introductory activity

Ask the children what a compliment is.
Ask them to suggest some compliments. If necessary give them some examples:
'I think you are great';
'You are always fair'.

Talk

Praise is paying God a compliment. It means telling him how good he is.
  Here is a poem from the Bible which does this.

  I will praise the Lord with all my being,
  I will never forget his kindness to me.
  He forgives me when I do wrong,
  He heals me when I am sick,
  He gives me strength like the eagle.
  God looks after the poor and the sad,
  He is gentle and loving,
  Very slow to anger but quick to love.
  He does not punish us as we deserve,
  Instead he removes our wrong to the farthest corners of the earth.
  His love is as big as the universe.
  He is as kind as a father to us because he knows how fragile we are.

(Adapted from Psalm 103)

Comment

Christians today still pay God compliments, they tell him how good he is when they pray. What sort of things do you think they say?

(Write some of them down, if you wish.)

Think about it

If you could choose, what would you like people to say to you? Think about it for a moment. Sometimes we find it hard to say nice things to other people; we feel a bit silly. It is worth making the effort because it means a lot to people.

Prayer

Thank you, God, for being loving and kind, faithful and just. Thank you for being all the good things we can think of.

F 5. Thanks

You will need:

A large piece of card (A3) to make
a thank-you card, some felt pens.

Introductory activity

Talk about the times when we say 'thank you'.

Introduce the subject of thank-you cards for Christmas and birthday presents.

Make a large thank-you card and decorate the front. (Leave the inside blank.)

Talk

Prayers are often about saying 'thank you'. Here is a thank-you poem from the Bible.

> Let's thank God for he is good,
> His love never ends.
> Let's thank God for being greater than anyone else.
> His love never ends.
> Let's thank God for being more powerful than anyone on earth.
> His love never ends.
> Let's thank God because he is wise.
> His love never ends.
> Let's thank God for making the sky and the sea.
> His love never ends.
> Let's thank God for making the sun, moon and stars.
> His love never ends.
> Let's thank God for everything.

(Adapted from Psalm 136)

Comment

When Christians pray they say 'thank you' to God for all he does. What do you think a Christian might want to put inside this thank-you card?

(Fill in the thank-you card with the children's suggestions.)

Think about it

Listen to this reading carefully and think about the words.
> We appreciate health only when we are sick. We are grateful for friendship when we are lonely. We notice love only when we are rejected. We appreciate strength when we are weak, and food when we are hungry. Help us, Father, to appreciate these things when we have them and to say 'thank you'.

Prayer

Lord, help us to remember to say 'thank you' and never take you or others for granted.

F 6. Asking

You will need:

Paper and a pen.

Introductory activity

Talk with the children about the things they would like for birthday or Christmas. Write a list.

Read this extract from 'King John's Christmas' by A.A.Milne, from *Now We Are Six*.

> King John was not a good man,
>   He lived his life aloof;
> Alone he thought a message out
>   While climbing up the roof.
> He wrote it down and propped it
>   Against the chimney stack:
> "TO ALL AND SUNDRY – NEAR AND FAR –
> F. CHRISTMAS IN PARTICULAR."
> And signed it not "Johannes R."
>   But very humbly, "JACK."
>
> "I want some crackers.
>   And I want some candy;
> I think a box of chocolates
>   Would come in handy;
> I don't mind oranges,
>   I do like nuts!
> And I SHOULD like a pocket-knife
>   That really cuts.
> And, oh! Father Christmas, if you love me at all,
> Bring me a big, red india-rubber ball!"

Talk

Some people think that prayer is just asking for things. When Christians pray they do ask God for things they need and they trust God to provide for them. Here is what Jesus said about asking:

'Don't worry about what you are going to eat and drink and wear. Look at the birds of the air, they are not worried, God feeds them. Look at the flowers, they are not anxious, yet even the king in his royal robes is not as beautiful as they are.

If God clothes the flowers which live for only a short time, how much more will he look after people!

Not even one sparrow falls to the ground without God knowing about it. He even knows the number of hairs on your head. God who cares for the sparrow cares even more about you.'

(Matthew 6:25–31, Luke 12:6, adapted)

Comment

Prayer is not just asking, it is not just giving God a list of all the things we want. Christians believe that God gives people what they need, not always what they ask for.

Prayer

Thank you, Father, that you know us so well that you know everything about us, all our wants and needs, all our hopes and dreams. Thank you that you love us enough to give us what we need. Help us to trust you for those things we really do need and not to worry about the rest.

F 7. Asking for Others

You will need:

A dish containing sand, some candles. Some water, as a safety measure.

Introductory activity

Explain that Christians often ask God to help other people. Not all asking is selfish, much of it is asking for others. They may be asking for someone to get better or to be given something they need.

Talk

Prayer includes asking for others. Here is an example of a prayer a Christian might pray:

Dear God, please help my friend Jane. Her Mum has gone into hospital and Jane is feeling very lonely and worried. May she feel your love for her and her family and may she know that you are with her and with her Mum in hospital. Give the doctors and nurses wisdom to use the gifts of healing which you have given them, and give them patience and strength in their difficult job. Be with Jane's Mum and make her better so that she can come home soon.

Comment

Not all prayer is spoken: many prayers are said silently. Sometimes Christians light a candle and the light and the smoke drifting upwards remind them of prayers going up to God. As the candle burns they think of the person who needs help. In Roman Catholic churches people light candles and say a prayer to God, often asking him to help someone else. In Lincoln Cathedral there are enormous pottery dishes full of sand; people light candles and put them in the dishes. Each candle stands for a prayer.

Make your own sand dish in assembly, but warn children not to light candles without an adult.

Think about it

Some of you might like to pray silently for a friend, while the candle burns. The rest can just sit quietly for a minute.

Prayer

Thank you, Father, that we can pray for our friends in need. Help us to remember others in our prayers.

F 8. Help!

You will need:

A torch with a flash button, paper and pens.

Introductory activity

On the paper write S O S in Morse code (three dots, three dashes, three dots). Explain what S O S means. Flash the message with the torch.

Talk about other distress signals, such as 'Mayday', dialling 999.

Talk with the children about whom they would ask for help if they were in trouble or danger.

Talk

Prayers can include asking for help when you are frightened, in trouble or in danger. They are S O S prayers. Here is a poem from the Bible in which someone is asking for help.

Help me, God!
I'm troubled and upset.
I'm exhausted with weeping.
Save me because you love me.
Each night I cry myself to sleep,
I soak my pillow with my tears.
My eyes are red and swollen,
I can hardly see.
I know you listen to me,
You hear my crying.
You will rescue me.

(Adapted from Psalm 6)

Comment

Asking for help is a normal part of prayer. Christians still ask God for help when they are in trouble, but they try to remember to thank him when he has helped them and not forget him when everything is all right.

Think about it

Think about a time when you needed help. Think about the people who helped you.

Prayer

Thank you, Father, that you always listen when we cry for help. Thank you also for the help that comes from other people.

F 9. Answering

You will need:

A large sheet of paper and a pen.

Introductory activity

Ask the children what nagging is. Make sure they realize it is more than being told off, that it is the same thing being said over and over again.

Write up some typical 'nags' on a large sheet of paper. How do children nag? How do parents nag?
Examples: Don't throw your coat on the floor. It's time to go to bed. You haven't done the washing-up yet. Can I have some sweets? Can I stay up late? Why can't I have a new bike?

Talk

Jesus told two stories about nagging to show what God is *not* like.

The friend at midnight

Late one night a man was woken up by a loud knocking on his door. Not knowing who it was, he shouted out, 'Who is it?'

It was his neighbour knocking frantically. 'A friend of mine has just arrived and I have no food to give him. Can you lend me three loaves?'

'No I can't,' said the man. 'The whole family are asleep and I am not getting up for that.'

The other man kept knocking at the door and eventually for the sake of peace and quiet, his neighbour got out of bed and gave him some bread.

The persistent widow

In a certain town lived a judge who was very strict and uncaring. In the same town lived a poor widow who kept coming to him and asking him to see that she was treated fairly. The judge refused to do anything about the poor widow's case, but the widow kept pestering him and after a while he said to himself, 'Although I don't care about this widow's situation, she is pestering me to death! I'll sort out her case so that she stops coming and annoying me with her demands.'

Comment

Jesus wanted to make people realize how eager God is to answer prayer. The man in the first story gave his neighbour some bread just to get rid of him. The judge gave in just to get some peace, not because he really cared about the widow being unfairly treated.

Jesus said that God is *not* like either of these people. He doesn't answer prayer because he has been nagged into doing it, he *wants* to answer prayer. Christians believe that God answers prayer, but not always by saying 'Yes', sometimes he says 'No' or 'Wait'.

Prayer

Thank you, Father, that you do answer prayer, and that you answer prayer willingly, not like the people in these stories.

F 10. Saying Sorry

You will need:

Some paper and a pen.

Introductory activity

Talk about when we say sorry and why. Ask the children for examples of things people say sorry for. Write some of them down.

Talk

Here is a 'saying sorry' prayer from the Bible.

I know I have done wrong, God.
Forgive me.
I know when I hurt others, I hurt you.
You were right to correct me.
I know you want us to do right,
and be truthful.
Give us the wisdom we need to
choose what is right.

Wash me and I shall be clean of all wrong.
Rub out my wrong and make me joyful again.
Don't leave me on my own.
Give me a new heart that wants to do what is right.
I'd give anything to make up for what I have done wrong,
But I know you don't need anything.
All you want is a repentant heart,
A person who is truly sorry and wants to change.

(Adapted from Psalm 51)

Comment

When Christians pray they say sorry to God for the things they have done wrong. They ask God to forgive them and they ask his help to change.

Think about it

Think about times when you have said sorry. Spend a little time thinking about how you say it and why you say it. Is it said because you really feel sorry or because you are made to say it?

Prayer

Thank you, Father, that you are a loving God who forgives those who are sorry and want to change.

Follow-up Work for the Classroom

1. Children could write out examples of different types of prayer as a creative writing exercise. Alternatively, you could make a 'communication' display and relate it to prayer.
2. Ask the children to copy out one of the Psalms from this section and decorate it appropriately.

G 1. *Forgiveness – What Is It?*

You will need:

Paper, a red pen and a black pen.

Introductory activity

Write the following in red on separate sheets of paper.
1. You owe the bank £10.
2. I owe you one pinch, two hits, three stamps on the foot and one punch, because that is what you did to me yesterday.

Talk

When you are an adult you get many bills through the post saying that you have to pay money for gas, electricity, water and so on. If you owe someone something it is called a debt. If you do not pay the money you owe, it is called 'going into the red' because the debt is sometimes written in red ink to show that it is owed and has yet not been paid. (Show them the debt of £10 written in red.)

Debts may not always be in money. If your friends are horrible to you, you might want to 'pay them back' in similar behaviour, like the person here. (Show them the behaviour bill written in red.) That is a different type of debt but it could also be written in red to show that it is a debt owed.

If you pay your debt and no longer owe any money your receipt is written in black. Forgiveness is like rubbing out the red and writing in black to show that the debt is not owed any more.

(Cross out your bill with the black pen and write 'Nothing to pay'.)

Comment

Forgiveness is about cancelling debts of behaviour and not insisting on doing back to people what they did to you.

Think about it

Think about a time when you have done something nasty to someone else.

I am going to tear up some paper, we will pretend it is a list of all the things people do wrong. Listen to the sound. Forgiveness is when someone tears up the list of all the things you have done wrong so that you can be friends again.

Prayer

Forgiveness is hard. It is hard to say sorry and it is hard to forgive others. Help us to say sorry and to forgive.

G 2. You Hit Me and I'll Hit You Back

You will need:

Some paper and a pen.

Introductory activity

Write down this saying from the Bible:
'An eye for an eye, a tooth for a tooth.'

Explain what the saying means.

Sometimes one person would start a fight and give someone a black eye; the other person would then feel that they could give the first person a black eye in return. The Bible made it plain that if one person knocked out a tooth, the other person could knock out only one tooth in return. You could only knock out one tooth for another, not two for one. The ideal was always forgiveness, as this story shows.

Story

Saul the king was jealous of David and wanted to kill him because he thought that David wanted to be king himself. Once when David was hiding in a cave, Saul entered it not knowing that David and his men were there. David saw Saul but Saul did not see David. His men urged David to kill Saul. 'He deserves it,' they said, 'after what he has done to you.'

'Kill the king? Never!' said David. He refused to touch Saul but he quietly crept up to him and cut a small piece from his cloak with a knife.

When Saul left the cave David came out and shouted to him, 'King Saul, why do you listen to all the lies people are spreading about me? I was in the cave you have just left – look, here is a piece of your cloak. I could have killed you but I don't want to pay you back for all the wrong you have done to me.'

Saul felt ashamed. 'Is that you David, my boy?' replied Saul. 'You are a better person than I am, you have been kind to me when I have been cruel to you. God bless you, one day you will be the king.

Comment

If David had killed Saul no one would have blamed him because Saul had tried to kill him first. It would have been only fair! But David went beyond being fair, he forgave Saul and let him live when he could have killed him very easily. Jesus said that people should not seek revenge, they should forgive even their enemies.

Prayer

Lord, hating is easier than loving. It's sometimes hard to love our friends, and we find it impossible to love our enemies without your help. Give us your love.

G 3. Bitterness and Revenge

You will need:

Your best coat or one that looks new.

Introductory activity

Show the children your best coat and say that it is better than anyone else's coat.

Talk about how other people react when someone boasts.

Story

Joseph was one of twelve brothers, he was one of the youngest. His father, Jacob, liked him more than his brothers, which was not fair. One day Jacob gave Joseph a special coat far better than anything his brothers had. This made Joseph's brothers very jealous. Why should their little brother be dressed better than they were? The more they thought about it the more jealous they became.

To make things worse, Joseph had some strange dreams. First he dreamt that all the sheaves of corn bowed down to him, then he dreamt that the sun and the moon and eleven stars bowed down to him. Joseph realized that one day he would be an important person and many people including his own family would kneel to him. When he told his family about these dreams, his brothers were really annoyed and they decided they could stand this spoilt child no longer. When they had Joseph alone they took off his new coat and dipped it in goat's blood and decided to tell their father that Joseph had been killed. They were going to leave Joseph to die down in a pit but instead they sold him to some slave merchants travelling to Egypt.

*When Joseph arrived in Egypt he was sold to a man called Potiphar. Joseph worked very hard and became a valued servant until one day he was falsely accused of attacking Potiphar's wife and he was thrown into prison. Joseph stayed there for many years, frightened and alone.

One day two men joined him in prison. Both men had strange dreams which troubled them and Joseph told them what they meant. One of the men was released and went back to work for the king. He forgot all about Joseph until some time later when the king had two strange dreams.

Joseph was called out of prison to unravel the king's nightmares. He told the king that his strange dreams meant that there would be seven years of good harvest in Egypt and seven years of bad harvest. Joseph suggested they collect grain in the good years and store them ready for the bad years.

The seven years of good harvest and the seven years of bad harvest happened, just as Joseph had said. Instead of being sent back to prison Joseph was put in charge of collecting the food and became one of the most important men in Egypt.

When the seven years bad harvest came no one in Egypt went hungry, everyone had enough to eat. In Canaan, the land where Joseph's family lived, times were hard and people had very little to eat. Jacob sent his sons to Egypt to buy grain from the Egyptians. Joseph's brothers came to Egypt to buy food but they did not recognize the little brother they had sold as a slave many years before.

Joseph wanted to be friends with his brothers again, but first he wanted to make sure they had changed. He asked a servant to plant a golden cup in one of the sacks of grain his brothers had bought. When the brothers were about to go, he called out 'Stop!' and accused them of stealing. Joseph went through all the sacks and found the golden cup in Benjamin's sack. The other brothers swore that Benjamin had not taken the cup, they protested that Benjamin was innocent. They offered to be slaves themselves rather than lose Benjamin. Joseph knew they were changed men and told them that he was their long-lost brother Joseph whom they had sold as a slave. Joseph forgave his brothers and invited them all to come and live in Egypt.

Comment

There was wrong on both sides in this story – Joseph was a spoilt child and the brothers tried to kill him and sold him as a slave. But Joseph changed as he grew up and he was willing to forgive his brothers. Broken friendships can be mended only when there is forgiveness and change.

Forgiveness does not always happen. Listen to the story again and see what might have happened if Joseph had not forgiven his brothers.

(Read the story above to the point marked * and then add this different ending.)

Joseph was so angry with his brothers that he swore he would get his own back one day. He was sold to a man called Potiphar and he worked hard so that he would win his freedom and one day return to Canaan and get his own back on his brothers. But his plans were ruined when he was falsely accused of attacking Potiphar's wife and was thrown in jail.

Joseph became bitter and hard. Once again he was suffering and he had done nothing wrong – life was so unfair. It was all his brothers' fault; one day he would have his revenge. While he was in jail he interpreted two men's dreams. Later, when the king had some bad dreams Joseph was sent for to interpret them. After telling the king what the dreams meant, Joseph was freed and given an important job. Soon, he thought, he would be able to deal with his brothers.

One day his brothers came begging for food. Joseph laughed, they did not even recognize their little brother. Joseph planted a golden cup in one of their grain sacks and had them arrested for theft. Now he put his plan into action, he would make them suffer as he had suffered. Joseph made them work as slaves, then he had them thrown into prison. He raised their hopes of freedom and then dashed them. He would make them feel what he had felt. Joseph got his revenge – he was important, wealthy and free, but he was lonely and bitter.

Think about it

Joseph made a choice. He chose to forgive. Think of times when you have needed to forgive someone.

Prayer

Teach us to forgive, as bitterness only ruins lives and destroys friendships.

G 4. Making It up

You will need:

A few flowers, a chocolate box (empty).

Introductory activity

Talk about having arguments and making it up and the 'tokens' that people give each other to show they want to make up. (Show them the chocolates and flowers.)

Story

This is a story from the Bible.

Jacob and Esau were twin brothers but they were not at all alike. Esau was big and strong and loved to go out hunting; Jacob was small and quieter and liked to stay at home. Esau was his father's favourite, but Jacob was his mother's favourite. Isaac, their father was old and nearly blind and knew that he would soon die. The time had come for him to pass on to Esau the special blessing that was passed from father to son. But Jacob decided that he wanted it, after all he was only a few minutes younger than his brother, so he and Rebecca, his mother, planned to trick Isaac.

Isaac told Esau to catch and prepare some food for a special meal. Esau was to bring the food to Isaac and when Isaac had eaten it he would give Esau his blessing. Rebecca heard this, so she killed two goats and cooked the meat and told Jacob to take it to Isaac. She also tied animal skin on to Jacob's arms so that they felt hairy, like Esau's.

Jacob took the food to Isaac, who was surprised that it was ready so quickly. He listened to his son's voice, it did not sound like Esau's so he felt his son's arms. The arms were hairy like Esau's so Isaac passed on the blessing, believing that he was giving it to Esau. The trick had worked – Jacob had stolen Esau's gift. But Jacob soon stopped rejoicing when Esau came home. His brother was so angry that Jacob had to run for his life and leave the home he loved.

Jacob was away for many years and during that time he changed. He wanted to return home but he did not know how Esau would react. Jacob had not seen his brother since the day he had tricked him and he wondered if Esau would ever forgive him. Before he went back Jacob sent presents of goats, camels, sheep and cattle. Esau not only accepted the presents, he ran to meet his brother and they hugged each other, each man crying with happiness that they had met again after so many years. Esau forgave his brother for Jacob was now a changed man.

Comment

Jacob wanted to make it up to Esau and to show he had changed he sent presents of cattle and other animals. Today people sometimes do something similar, they send flowers or chocolates to show they want to make it up. But sending flowers and chocolates is no good if it does not mean anything; it should be a way of saying sorry and showing that you want to change.

Prayer

Father, help us to show we are sorry not only by the little things we do but by a change in our behaviour.

G 5. Forgive Us as We Forgive Others

You will need:

Some items to bargain with (optional).

Introductory activity

Talk about striking bargains with friends. For example, someone might say, 'I'll let you play with my car if you let me play with your game, that's only fair.' Say that it would not be fair if Jane let Kate play with her games, but Kate never let Jane play with hers.

Ask the children to suggest the types of bargains they might make.

Talk

One day Jesus's disciples asked him to teach them how to pray, so he taught them this prayer. (Use the form of the prayer your children know if they know the Lord's prayer; if not use the version below.)

Our Father in heaven:
May your holy name be honoured;
May your kingdom come;
May your will be done on earth as it is in heaven.
Give us today the food we need.
Forgive us the wrongs we have done,
As we forgive the wrongs that others have done to us.
Do not bring us to hard testing,
But keep us safe from the Evil One.

(Matthew 6:9-13, Good News Bible version)

The piece of this prayer we are interested in today is: *'Forgive us the wrongs we have done, as we forgive the wrongs that others have done to us.'*

If you look closely it seems like a bargain. God is making a type of bargain. 'If you forgive other people the wrong they do to you,' says God, 'I will forgive the wrong that you do.' That's only fair. People cannot expect to be forgiven themselves and yet never forgive anyone else.

Comment

Forgiveness is never easy, but sometimes it is easier to forgive others if we look at some of the things we have done wrong and realize that we all make mistakes. Forgiveness is the best solution in an imperfect world.

Think about it

Think about your friends and the things they do that annoy you. Next time you moan about your friends think of some of the things you do wrong.

Prayer

Father, help us to forgive other people, who are as imperfect as we are.

G 6. *Don't Stop Forgiving*

$$2 \times 2$$

$$4 \times 2$$

$$10 \times 10$$

You will need:

Paper and pens.

Introductory activity

Do some basic multiplication sums. Start with very simple ones and move on to more difficult ones. With infants do this practically.

Story

One day Jesus's friend Peter asked Jesus how many times he should forgive someone. Peter probably expected Jesus to say 'once' or 'twice' but Jesus said 'seventy times seven'. Peter was shocked because when he went away to do the sum, the answer was 490. Jesus had told Peter to forgive his enemy 490 times.

Comment

Jesus did not really mean that Peter had to forgive his enemy 490 times and then he could get his own back on the 491st occasion. Jesus used this big sum just as a way of saying that you should never stop forgiving your enemy. He could equally well have said 'ninety times nine' or 'a hundred times ten'.

Think about it

It is hard to imagine forgiving someone when they hurt you time and time again or when people do something very bad.

In the Second World War, when Coventry was bombed someone took some burnt wood from the ruins of the Cathedral and made a cross and carved on it the words 'Father Forgive'. These are the words Jesus said when he was dying. Think about that simple cross with those words written on it.

Prayer

Father, it is hard to carry on forgiving. Give us your love for others that will help us to forgive even when we feel we can't.

G 7. Those Who Are Forgiven Much, Love Much

Introductory activity

Talk with the children about looking after visitors. Ask them what sort of things they do when a visitor arrives, particularly if the person has had a long journey.

Story

In Jesus's time it was the custom to wash visitors' feet when they arrived. One day Jesus went to the house of Simon the Pharisee for a meal. While they were eating and talking a woman arrived, she sat down at Jesus's feet and began to cry. She washed Jesus's feet with her tears and dried them with her hair. She poured precious, expensive perfume over his feet. Simon watched this and thought to himself, 'If this man were really God's special king he would know what sort of woman this is, he would know she is a bad woman and he would not let her touch him.'

Jesus knew what Simon was thinking. 'When I came to your house you did not welcome me or give me water to wash my feet. This woman has welcomed me and washed my feet with her tears. I know she has been bad in the past but she is trying to show that she wants to change.' Jesus looked at the woman and told her that her sins were forgiven and she went away.

Jesus explained, 'Sometimes people who have done a lot wrong and are sorry find it easier to forgive others because they know what it means to be forgiven. Those who have been forgiven a lot love others more than those who have been forgiven only a little.'

Comment

There is an old saying that great sinners sometimes make great saints. This woman had done a lot wrong but she had shown that she was sorry and wanted to change.

Think about it

Some people think they are too bad to be a friend of God, but some of Jesus's friends had a very bad record. Paul used to capture Christians and put them in prison. Peter once pretended that he never knew Jesus. Anyone can be forgiven if they really want to change.

Prayer

When we find it hard to forgive, teach us to look at ourselves and remember what it is like to be forgiven.

G 8. Paying a Debt

You will need:

Mock slave-auction poster on a large sheet of paper.
Copies of the first verse of 'Amazing Grace'.

> Amazing grace,
> How sweet the sound
> That saved a wretch like me.
> I once was lost but now am found
> Was bound but now am free.

> **SLAVE AUCTION**
> To be held in the Market Place on Saturday 9th November 1791. Newly arrived slaves from Africa for sale.

Introductory activity

Hold up the slave-auction poster and explain what a slave auction was.

Arrange a mock slave auction, if you wish, using staff or children chosen with care.

Story

When he was only a boy of eleven John Newton went to sea. He lead an adventurous life as a sailor and faced many dangers. John was rough and hard and for a living he sold people. He captured them on the west coast of Africa and put them in slave ships bound for America where they were sold as slaves to work on plantations. The conditions on the boats were so terrible for the slaves that many died on the voyage. The life waiting for them in America was even worse – they were treated by some people as little better than animals.

One day John Newton was caught in a great storm at sea. He thought he was going to die. Then he started to pray, he asked God to save him from drowning. John did not die for the storm died down, and inside he knew that he had changed. He had begun to believe in God. Very slowly his faith grew, he did not change all at once. Slowly he began to realize how terrible slavery was and he was ashamed that he had once captured and sold slaves. He spent the rest of his life trying to free slaves for he knew he had a terrible debt to pay.

John Newton supplied information to men such as William Wilberforce to help them in their fight against the slave trade. In 1807 the slave trade was finally stopped in the British Empire. Slaves could no longer be bought and sold and in 1833 all the slaves were freed in those countries. John Newton had paid his debt.

Comment

John Newton wrote a hymn which is very well known – it is called 'Amazing Grace'. Grace here is another word for love. John calls himself a wretch because of what he did. He describes himself as blind because he was blind to other people's suffering, and he says he was bound or chained like a slave because he was chained with wrong or sin.

You could arrange for some children to play 'Amazing Grace' on their recorders, while everyone else sings the first verse. (See music on p.79.)

Think about it

Imagine being a slave and having chains on your ankles. Imagine being sold and not knowing what your master would be like.

Prayer

Thank you, Father, for the story of John Newton who was not only forgiven but tried to put right the wrong he had caused.

G 9. Treat Others as You Would Like To Be Treated

You will need:

It's not fair by A. Harper, published by Puffin (optional).

Introductory activity

Talk with the children about situations which are unfair. If you have the book *It's not fair* read it to the children.

Story

Here is a story from the Bible about someone who was very unfair.

Once there was a king who was owed a lot of money by his servants. As the king went through his account book he noticed that one servant owed him millions of pounds. The servant was brought in and the king told him to pay back the money he owed. The servant said that he could not pay, so the king ordered that he and his family should be sold as slaves. The servant pleaded with the king, who then felt sorry for him and told him he did not have to pay back the debt.

As the servant was leaving the palace he saw someone who owed him a few pounds and he immediately demanded that the man pay him. The man pleaded with him but the servant would not listen and he had the man thrown into prison.

The other servants told the king about this. The king was furious; he sent for the ungrateful servant and said, 'I forgave you your massive debt, yet you could not let someone else off paying a few pounds!' The king sent for the guards and the unforgiving servant was thrown into prison.

Comment

The story about the debtor who did not forgive is a story of unfairness. He had been forgiven so much and yet he could not forgive the man who owed him only a little.

Think about it

Next time you have an argument with someone, say to yourself, 'If I was in that person's situation how would I like to be treated?'

Prayer

Thank you that you forgive us so much. Help us to remember that when people wrong us.

G 10. A Man Who Changed

You will need:

Some money (real or toy).

Introductory activity

Explain what taxes are to the children.

Call out a group of *five* pupils and give each one some money. Make an announcement that the government is going to tax everyone 10p. Add on 5p for yourself and collect the taxes, counting up how much money you have made for yourself. Explain to the children that this is a form of stealing.

Story

Zacchaeus was a tax collector in the town of Jericho. He was also a thief for he increased the amount people had to pay and kept some for himself. He was hated by all the people of Jericho, which was hardly surprising.

One day Zacchaeus heard that Jesus was visiting the town. A crowd gathered along the road but Zacchaeus could not see Jesus for he was too short and he was stuck at the back of the crowd. He tried to push forward but the people just elbowed him to the back of the crowd. 'Jesus won't want to see you,' they said. Zacchaeus was determined to see Jesus so he climbed a tree and watched him from there.

As Jesus walked through the town he stopped and looked up at Zacchaeus, 'Come down, Zacchaeus, I want to stay at your house today.' Zacchaeus climbed down as fast as he could and welcomed Jesus into his house. The people moaned, 'It's disgusting Jesus staying with a bad man like Zacchaeus, everyone knows he is a thief.'

A little while later Zacchaeus emerged from his house and said to the people, 'I will give half of everything I have to the poor and if I have cheated anybody I will give back four times what I owe him.'

Comment

We do not know what Jesus said to him or why Zacchaeus changed, but we do know that he was sorry and wanted to make it up to people. He decided to give back four times what he had stolen. That means if he stole 5p he would give back 20p.

Zacchaeus changed his behaviour, which helped people to forgive him.

Prayer

Thank you for the example of Zacchaeus who changed completely on the inside. May we show by our behaviour what we are like on the inside.

Follow-up Work for the Classroom

1. Talk with the children about situations involving forgiveness, and particularly the fine line between forgiveness and exploitation.
2. Make a story cube, in which different stories from this section are mounted on a covered box and suspended or displayed.
3. The story of Zacchaeus can be mimed by the children as the teacher tells the story.
4. Get the children to illustrate various aspects of forgiveness, using the stories in this section.

AMAZING GRACE

H 1. Christmas Decorations 1 (Evergreens)

You will need:

Some evergreen foliage, ribbon, a plastic P.E. hoop, sellotape, scissors.

Introductory activity

Show the evergreens to the children and explain that they are from trees which keep their leaves in the winter. They do not shed all their leaves in the autumn as some trees do.

Talk about the use of evergreen leaves as Christmas decorations. They can be tied into bunches with ribbons and hung up, or more often they are tied into rings and hung on doors or in windows. If you wish, you can tie the leaves to a hoop with string or sellotape and decorate with ribbons.

Ask some children to help you make bunches of evergreens for display in the hall.

Talk

Evergreen leaves are used at Christmas. They can act as a sign of God and his love. As the tree is always green, so God is always there. The leaves are tied into a circle which never ends, just as God and his love never end.

(Show the children a circle and ask them to find its beginning or its end.)
When you see a circle of evergreens this year remember what they can mean.

Think about it

Listen quietly to this reading and think about it.

Leaves fall and wither,
The trees stand bare,
Their bony hands reaching for the sky.
The fir tree stays green.
Its needles sharp,
An arrow pointing to God.

Prayer

Thank you, Father, for the sign of the evergreens which reminds us of your unending love.

H 2. Christmas Decorations 2 (Tinsel)

You will need:

Some tinsel.
A Christmas tree (optional). The next four assemblies explore the meaning behind some of the decorations on the tree. You might like to have a Christmas tree to which you add something each day.

Introductory activity

Show the children some tinsel and ask what it is used for at Christmas. Put it round the tree.

Talk

Here is a legend which explains why tinsel is used at Christmas.

When King Herod heard that a new baby king had been born he was very worried, he thought the new king would grow up and take over his kingdom. The more Herod thought about it the more angry he became. He decided that he could not allow this baby to live so he sent his soldiers to Bethlehem to kill every child who was two years old and under. Joseph had already been warned by God to escape with Mary and Jesus, so they were not in Bethlehem when the soldiers arrived, they were hiding in a cave in a hill nearby.

Inside the cave it was bitterly cold. A spider saw the family and decided to help. Carefully the spider wove his best web over the mouth of the cave to help keep out the wind. Round and round the spider went until the cave mouth was completely covered in a fine web of silk. As the night drew on it got colder and colder and the web became covered with sparkling frost. Herod's soldiers had done their awful work in Bethlehem and now they started to scour the hillsides for anyone who had escaped. They walked by the cave entrance which was closed in a thick web covered in frost. Inside Mary and Joseph could hear the soldiers and they held their breath in fear.

'They can't be in there,' said one of the soldiers. 'Look at this spider's web, it hasn't been disturbed.'

The soldiers moved on, leaving the baby Jesus unharmed. Not only had the spider tried to keep them warm, but it had saved their lives as well.

Comment

This legend tells why tinsel is used at Christmas – it is a reminder of the spider's web covered in frost. This is not a true story but there is some truth in it. Though there were people like Herod who wanted to get rid of Jesus, there were also those like the shepherds, the wise men and, in this story, a humble spider who welcomed him.

Prayer

Thank you, Father, for the story of the spider who did the only thing it could to help save Jesus from the soldiers.

(**Note:** In Islam a similar story is told about Muhammad seeking refuge in a cave. Muslim children will be familiar with that story.)

H 3. Christmas Decorations 3
(The fairy on the Christmas tree)

You will need:

Two dolls - a fairy and an angel.
A copy of the Christmas story.

Introductory activity

Hold up the fairy and the angel. Ask the children where these dolls normally sit on the tree. Explain the difference between the two dolls: the fairy is a fictional character from stories, the angel is a messenger from God. (Some children might like to come to the front and examine the dolls).
Read the Christmas story and ask the children to stop you when they hear the fairy in the story.

Talk

There are no fairies in the Christmas story, but there is an angel, or rather, a lot of angels. The fairy is really a mistake. The next time you see a fairy on a Christmas tree remember that it is a mistake and there should be an angel sitting there to remind people of the angels in the Christmas story.

We'll put the angel on our Christmas tree. The angel sits on top of the tree because he has a message to tell everyone, that God's special king is born. Can you remember the angel's exact message from the Christmas story?

Think about it

Think about your Christmas tree at home. Try to remember whether you have a fairy or an angel on it.

Prayer

May we remember this Christmas the angels in the story and the message they proclaimed of peace on earth and good will to everyone.

H 4. Christmas Decorations 4 (Stars)

You will need:

Some cardboard templates of stars, scissors, card, Blu-Tak or a hole punch and some ribbon.
An overhead projector and a piece of paper with a lot of small holes in.
A recording of a carol such as 'See amid the winter's snow'.

Introductory activity

Cut out some simple stars using the templates. Ask the children to help you. Stick them on the wall with Blu-Tak or punch a hole through them and hang them on the tree. As you make the stars talk about the star appearing in the Christmas story.

Talk

Stars are hung on the Christmas tree to remind us of the star that led the wise men to Bethlehem. There are millions of stars in the sky, but to Christians this is a very special one and in pictures it is often drawn bigger than all the rest.

   The stars used in decorations also remind Christians that Jesus helped his Father to make the world at the very beginning of time. The person who made the stars slept underneath them as a baby.

Think about it

Look at the night sky we have made and listen to the carol.
Think about the words.

Make a 'night sky' with the overhead projector and play the carol.

Prayer

Thank you, Father, for the star that led the wise men and for the many stars that God created.

H 5. Christmas Decorations 5 (Fairy Lights)

You will need:

Some fairy lights.

Introductory activity

Put the lights on the tree and turn them on. Ask the children why we have lights on the tree.

Ask them what other sorts of lights we have and what they are for.
Examples: torches, light bulbs, lighthouses, cat's-eyes.

Talk

Jesus was called 'the Light of the World'. Christians believe he brings the light of love into a world dark with sadness and wrong. Here is what the Bible says:
(The words in brackets have been added to help the children's understanding.)

The people who walked in the darkness (of wrong) have seen a great light.
They used to live in the shadow but now the light (of love and life) is shining on them.

He brings the bright light (of God's love) to mankind. It is a light that shines in darkness and the darkness (of evil) shall never put it out.

I am the light of the world. Whoever follows me will not live in the darkness (of wrong) but will have the light of life (and love).

Comment

Next time you see fairy lights on a tree, remember the Christian belief about Jesus as 'the Light of the World'.

Think about it

Look at the fairy lights for a moment while the reading about the light of the world is read again. Think carefully about the words.
(Repeat the last quotation.)

Prayer

Thank you, Father, for this celebration of Christmas when Jesus came to bring light and love to the world. Help us to be lights too.

H 6. Advent Ring 1

You will need:

A cake board or circular metal tray or shallow cake tin, some sprigs of greenery (holly is normally used), plasticine, a large white candle and four red candles (to be used in the next five assemblies).
Some water, as a safety measure.

Note: If you wish, a small part of the Christmas story can be read each day to supplement these assemblies or the whole story can be read at the beginning or the end.

Introductory activity

Explain that the four weeks before Christmas are called Advent and it is the time when Christians get ready on the inside to welcome Jesus at Christmas. Some Christians make a special Advent ring to help them get ready.

Make the Advent ring with the help of the children. First make a circle of cones, ribbon bows and leaves, attaching them to the tray with plasticine (warm it first to make it stick). If using a cake tin tie a ribbon round it. Place one of the red candles in the circle, securing it with a large piece of plasticine.

Talk

The first candle stands for the Prophets. Prophets were people who told others about God and also spoke about what was going to happen in the future. Many prophets spoke about a very special king who would be sent by God. This special king would be just and fair, and he would bring peace and love.

Here are some of the things the prophets said:

A child has been born to us,
A son has been given,
He will rule the people.
He will be called: Wonderful, Counsellor,
The Mighty God, the Everlasting Father, the Prince of Peace.
There will be no end to his rule and the peace that he brings.
(Isaiah 9:6-7)

He will settle arguments between the nations. They shall beat their swords into ploughs and their spears into gardening tools. Nations shall not fight each other, nor shall they learn war any more.
(Micah 4:3-4)

The first candle is lit on the Sunday four weeks before Christmas and some of the writings of the Prophets in the Bible are read to remind Christians that people had been waiting for a special king for many years.

Think about it

As we light the candle look at the flame and think about how hard it must have been to wait. (Afterwards put the candle out.)

Prayer

For the Prophets who told people that you would send a special king, we praise you, God. They faithfully spoke of the king you would send, but they never saw him themselves.

(**Note:** The candles can be lit under adult supervision but must be blown out before they burn low and catch the decorations.)

H 7. Advent Ring 2

You will need:

The second red candle and some plasticine.
Some water, as before.

Introductory activity

Ask a child to place the second red candle in the ring.

Remind them briefly what the first candle stood for.

Talk

This candle is the John the Baptist candle, it is lit on the third Sunday before Christmas. John the Baptist was Jesus's cousin and he tried to prepare people for Jesus's coming. He told people to be sorry for the things they had done wrong and to change. To show that they had changed and were sorry for the wrong they had done, John 'baptized' them in the River Jordan. That means he lowered them under the water and then lifted them out and the people said they were sorry for all they had done wrong and they wanted to change. The washing on the outside was like a sign that people wanted to be clean of wrong on the inside.

Some Churches still have this special ceremony where people are baptized by being lowered under water to show that they want to change. Some of these Churches are called 'Baptist' Churches.

Lots of people listened to John and asked God to help them change. They waited and looked for the special king who they knew would come soon.

Think about it

Today we shall light two candles. Look at them and think about how you get ready for Christmas. Christians get ready by thinking about the things they want to change inside themselves. In this way they will be ready to welcome Jesus at Christmas.
(Put the candles out.)

Prayer

John the Baptist called people to get ready for your coming. May we be ready to welcome you this Christmas.

H 8. Advent Ring 3

You will need:

The third red candle and some plasticine.
Some water, as before.

Introductory activity

Ask a child to add the third candle to the ring.

Remind them of the meaning of the previous candles.

You could ask if there are any children called Mary or have Mary in their name (e.g. Rosemary). If you wish, ask one of these children to light the candles later on in the assembly.

Talk

This candle stands for Mary, Jesus's mother.
The Mary candle is lit to remind Christians how Mary got ready for Jesus's arrival. What sort of preparations do you think she might have made for the coming of a baby?
When Mary was told by the Angel Gabriel that she was going to have a son who would be God's special king she was very happy. This is what she said when she was given the news:

Inside I am really happy,
From now on everyone will know how happy I am.
God has done so much for me.
He is always gentle and forgiving with those who love and respect him.
He humbles the proud people,
But those who are poor and needy he looks after.
He fills the empty stomachs of the hungry and he always keeps his promises.

(Adapted from the Magnificat)

Think about it

As we light the third candle look at it and think about Mary getting ready for the baby. What would have been her hopes and her fears?
(Put the candles out.)

Prayer

Thank you, Father, for the example of Mary who believed your promise and got ready to welcome Jesus.

H 9. Advent Ring 4

You will need:

The fourth red candle and some plasticine.
Some water, as before.

Introductory activity

Ask a child to add the final red candle to the ring.

Remind them of the meaning of the first three candles.

Talk

The fourth red candle is lit on the last Sunday before Christmas. It is the candle of God's people, or the candle of hope. Christians remember that once Jesus came to earth as a baby, and they believe that one day he will return as a king. This is the candle of hope that one day Jesus will come back and finally wipe out all wrong.

Hope is something very uncertain in our language. We say things like, 'I hope it will not rain' or 'I hope I can have a new bike'.
(Ask the children for other suggestions of things they hope for.)

When Christians use the word 'hope' about something God has promised they believe that it will really happen. You might *hope* for a new bike but you don't *know* for sure because it is up to your parents. When people hope that God will do as he promised, it is a certain hope because Christians believe that he is powerful enough to carry out his promises and he wants to do so.

Think about it

(Light the fourth candle.) Look at the candles.
Think about hope for the future and the things about the earth that need changing.

Prayer

Thank you, Father, for the candle of God's people, the candle of hope. Thank you for that promise that Jesus will one day return.

H 10. Advent Ring 5

You will need:

The white candle and some plasticine.
Some water, as before.

Introductory activity

Place the large white candle in the centre of the Advent ring.

Briefly recall the meaning of all the candles.

Talk

The white candle is lit on Christmas morning. This candle stands for Jesus the king. Jesus is king even though he was born in a stable.

The circle of evergreens is the everlasting circle of God's love. Christians believe that God's love never ends.

The candles are the lights of life, love and hope. The centre candle is Jesus himself, the 'light of the world'.

Sometimes there is a sign on the Advent candle. It is Alpha (Α) and Omega (Ω), the first and last letters of the Greek alphabet. This represents the Christian belief that Jesus came at the first Christmas and will come again one day. Christians believe he was there at the beginning of the world and will be there at the end.

Think about it

Look at all the candles and think of the meaning of each one.

Prayer

Help us to remember the Christmas story as we celebrate Christmas this year. May the decorations remind us of the true meaning of this celebration.

Follow-up Work for the Classroom

1. Make a collage of an Advent ring using pieces of fabric.
2. You might like to follow up the meaning of different Christmas customs by reading to younger children from *Haffertee's First Christmas* by J. and J. Perkins, published by Lion.